ATLAS OF MODERN CLOTHING

Marina Madzhugina

ATLAS OF MODERN CLOTHING

From the Trench Coat to the Sweatshirt

HOAKI

HOAKI

Hoaki Books, S.L.
C/ Ausiàs March, 128
08013 Barcelona, Spain
T. 0034 935 952 283
F. 0034 932 654 883
info@hoaki.com
www.hoaki.com

hoakibooks

Atlas of Modern Clothing:
From the Trench Coat to the Sweatshirt

ISBN: 978-84-17656-60-7

Copyright © 2022 Hoaki Books, S.L. for the
English edition
Copyright © 2020 Art Lebedev Studio
Copyright © Martina Madzhugina
Original title: *От тренчкóта до свитшóта:
атлас современной одежды*

Author: Marina Madzhugina
Translation: Hoaki Books
Proofreading: Katherine Kirby with the
collaboration of Evgenia Shkuratova
Art director: Artemy Lebedev
Webmasters: Anna Golovina and Andrei Ushnurtsev
Illustrator: Marina Madzhugina
Assistant illustrator: Alexandra Baranovskaya
Editor: Katerina Andreeva
Fact-checker: Ekaterina Komarova
Manager: Svetlana Kalinnikova

D.L.: B 9782-2022
Printed in China

About the author

Marina Madzhugina graduated from the Institute of Design and Technology at Omsk State Technical University (Russia) with a degree in costume design. She has worked at her *alma mater* since 2013, teaching students who want to become stylists and image-makers. She is the winner of the Fashion Formula Competition (Omsk), the Local Style Competition for Young Fashion Designers (Voronezh) and the Russian Silhouette Contest (Sochi, Moscow). Over her career, she has developed a unique method to compile a basic assortment of clothing, which became the basis for this atlas.

About the book

This atlas is a detailed journey into the design and characteristics of modern outerwear, tops and trousers. In it, drawings show key details, list traditional materials, and use vivid stylised illustrations to demonstrate clothing 'on the model'. The book is sure to be a wonderful source of inspiration and a useful tool for artists and designers working in the fashion and costume industries, and will also interest anyone who is passionate about fashion and style.

Table of Contents

A note from the author

A toolkit for fashion enthusiast and professionals

Dear readers,
The atlas in your hands is intended for practicing garment designers and anyone with a genuine interest in fashion. I am sure it will be no less interesting for those who study the history of costumes and dress.

The atlas consists of three overarching sections: Outerwear, Tops/Dresses and Trousers/Skirts.

Each illustrated spread is strictly structured and divided into two areas: the first contains a detailed drawing and a brief summary of the characteristics of the garment, while the second contains a stylised image.

Alternate names are provided, and, generally, the country or place of origin of the garment and the key details that define it are indicated.

You can use the atlas in different ways, it all depends on your personal preferences and needs.

Depending on the projects you are working on and professional requirements, this book will be a valuable tool to spark creative solutions to garment-making problems or simply inspire the reader when choosing an outfit for the day.

I sincerely hope this atlas helps designers in their work, no matter what creative method of designing garments they use - inversion, analogy, empathy, fantasy, creation of new combinations, morphological analysis or something else.

Here's to creative inspiration,
Марина Маджугина

Coats

Classic single-breasted coat

Long lined coat with a single-breasted fastening.

Classic collar with lapels

Single-welt chest pocket

Concealed clasps or visible buttons

Darts

Horizontal or slant pockets

3 to 5 buttons

Vent

Wool * Broadcloth * Tweed * Cady * Cashmere * Bouclé * Cotton

Double-breasted coat

Long lined coat with a double-breasted fastening.

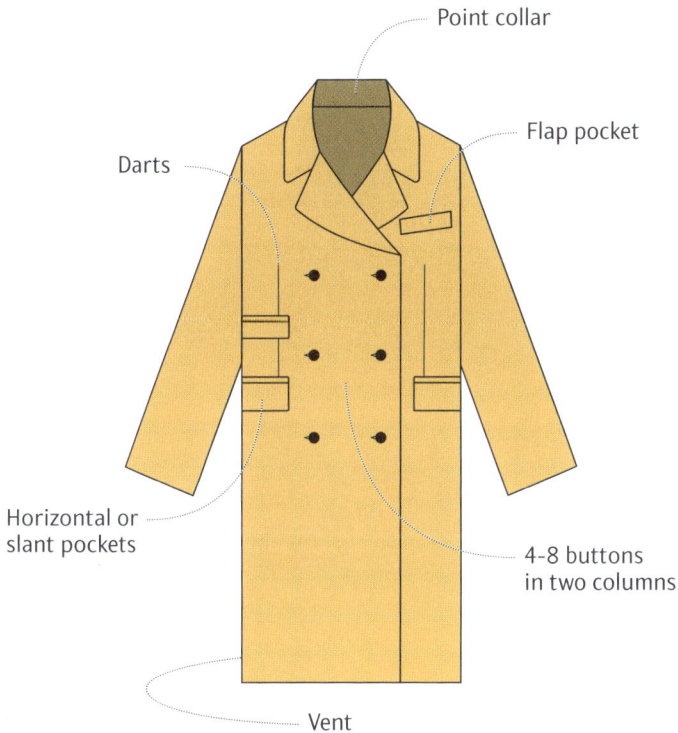

Point collar

Flap pocket

Darts

Horizontal or
slant pockets

4-8 buttons
in two columns

Vent

Wool * Broadcloth * Tweed * Cady * Cashmere * Bouclé * Cotton

Greatcoat

Historically used as military uniforms in many different countries.

Point Collar

Metal buttons

Epaulettes

Inverted pleat
at the back

2-button strap
at back for a
fitted silhouette

Turn-up cuffs

Flap pockets

Double- or single-
breasted fastening

Vent

Wool * Broadcloth * Cashmere

Frock coat

Originally a men's riding coat called a redingote.

Wide, flat collar, cape or lapels

Fitted silhouette

Straight, narrow cuffed sleeves

Vertical pockets

Double breasted

Flared Clasp

Waisted cut

Wool * Broadcloth

Ulster

A working daytime overcoat with a cape and sleeves.

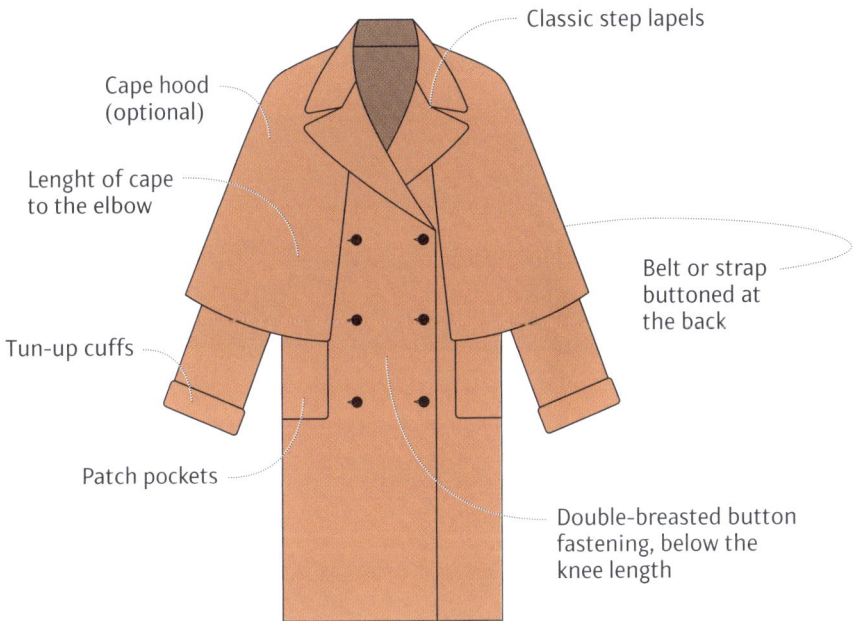

Classic step lapels

Cape hood
(optional)

Lenght of cape
to the elbow

Belt or strap
buttoned at
the back

Tun-up cuffs

Patch pockets

Double-breasted button
fastening, below the
knee length

∗ Donegal tweed ∗

Polo coat

Originally worn by polo players to warm up between matches.

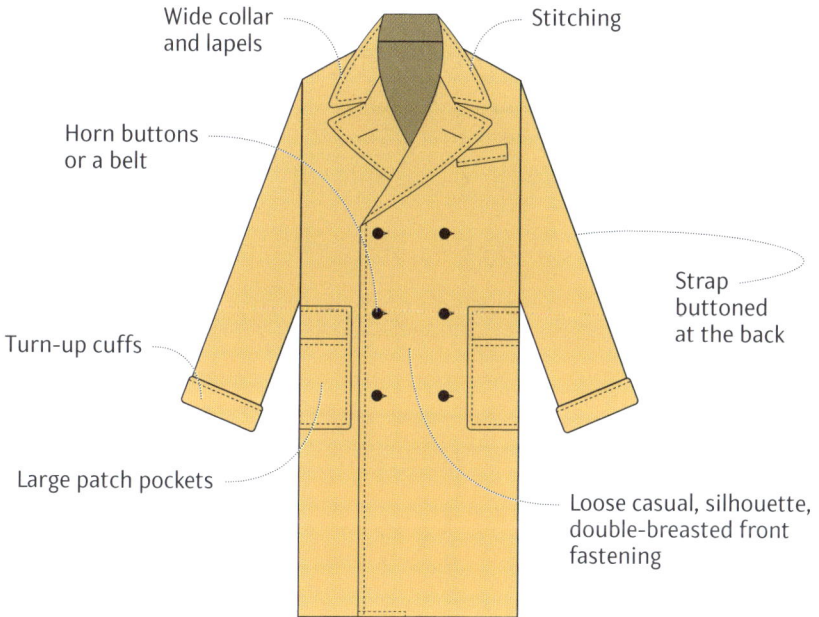

Wide collar
and lapels

Stitching

Horn buttons
or a belt

Strap
buttoned
at the back

Turn-up cuffs

Large patch pockets

Loose casual, silhouette,
double-breasted front
fastening

* Camel hair *

Covert coat

Originally a riding coat.

Covert cloth (tweed)
or velvet collar ·············   ············· Step lapels

                                                            ············· Fly front

3-4 front pockets ·············

4-5 rows of stitches
on cuffs and
hemline fastening   ············· Single-breasted

                                                            ············· Knee-length

* Covert cloth *

Mod coat

A classic single-breasted coat with step lapels.

Step lapels .... Red lining

Flap pockets ....

.... Fly fastening

³/₄ length

* Wool *

Balmacaan

A loose, full overcoat with raglan sleeves,
originally made of rough woollen cloth.

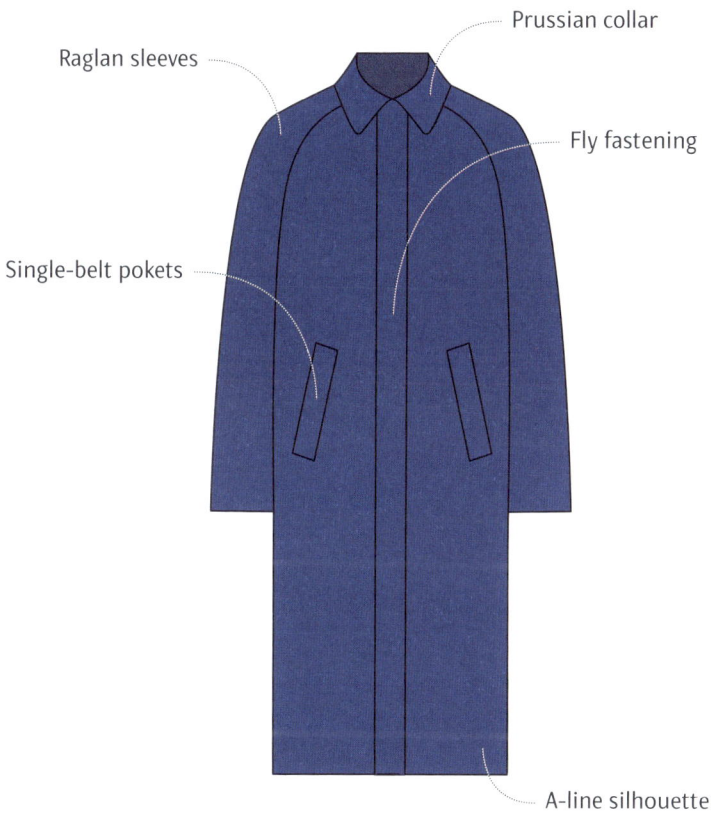

Prussian collar

Raglan sleeves

Fly fastening

Single-belt pokets

A-line silhouette

Thermal, waterproof lambswool * Tweed * Gabardine

Pea coat

Also called a pilot jacket, worn by European and US sailors.

Wide collars/lapels

Large buttons with images of anchors

Vertical pockets with or without flaps

Double-breasted front

Short length

Dark blue

∗ Heavy Melton cloth (wool) ∗

Duffel coat

A coat used by the British Royal Navy in the late 1800s.

Lined in hood woolly tartan

Bucket or pancake hood

Neck strap

Square yoke

Toggle fastenings

Leather straps

Flap patch pockets

Single-breasted front

Dark blue   Camel   Black

∗ Windproof Melton cloth, waterproof Duffel wool ∗

Cocoon coat

Unstructured with an ovoid shape.

Dropped shoulders, voluminous sleeves

Rounded, egg-like shape, similar to a cocoon

Unstructured silhouette

Narrower at the hem

Wool * Broadcloth * Tweed * Cady * Cashmere * Bouclé * Cotton

Three-quarter coat

Lightweight A-line coat with varying details.

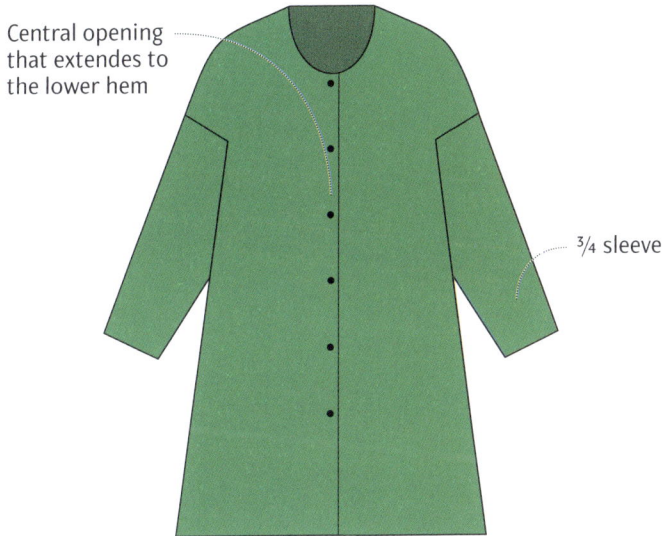

Central opening
that extendes to
the lower hem

³/4 sleeve

Fine wool * Broadcloth * Silk * Velvet * Crushed velvet

Swing coat

Also called a swagger coat. Varying lengths and details.

Raglan sleeves

Flared sleeves

Cut to flare
at the back

Trapeze silhouette

Loose
fitting cut

Wool * Broadcloth * Tweed * Cady * Cashmere * Bouclé

Poncho

A sort of cape that varies in colour, finish, and ornamentation.

Opening in the middle
for the head

Rectangular
piece of fabric

No sleeves

Wool * Broadcloth * Tweed * Cady * Cashmere * Bouclé * Cotton

43

Duster

A coat originally designed to protect horsemen from dust and rain.

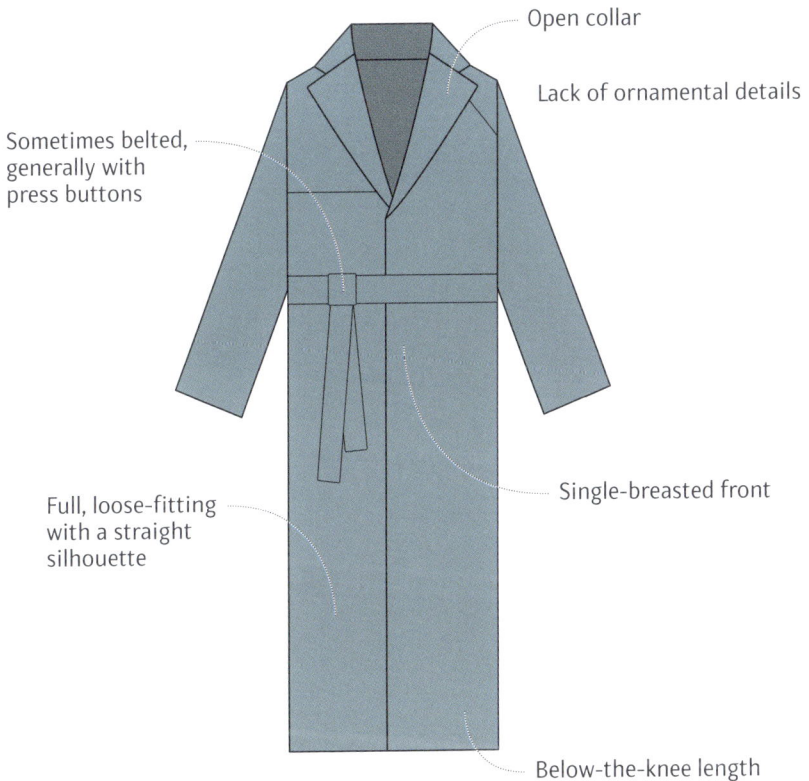

Open collar

Lack of ornamental details

Sometimes belted,
generally with
press buttons

Single-breasted front

Full, loose-fitting
with a straight
silhouette

Below-the-knee length

Suiting fabric ∗ Oilcloth ∗ Waterproof waxed cotton
Silk ∗ Viscose

Raincoats

Cape coat

Protective gear often worn by soldiers.

Multiple necklines: collar, a hood, or none at all

Imitation sleeves set-in or raglan

Various details

No actual sleeves

Slits for the hands

Loose, free fit

Single-breasted or double-breasted front

* Windproof, waterproof dense wool *

Inverness cape

A long coat with a cape instead of sleeves.

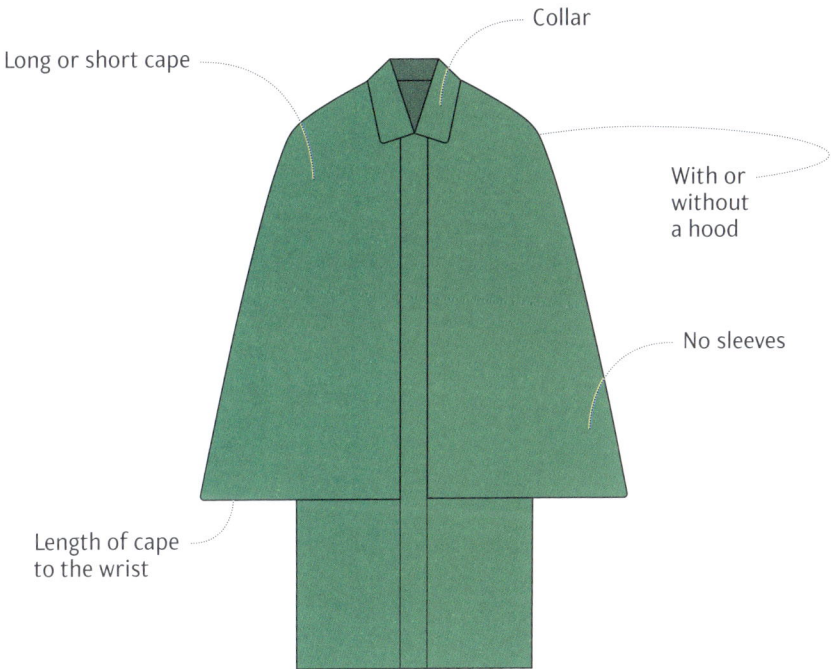

Collar

Long or short cape

With or without a hood

No sleeves

Length of cape to the wrist

Windproof, waterproof dense wool * Tweed

Trench coat

Military coat used in the trenches of WWI.

Neck strap

Collars / lapels

Shoulder straps

1 or 2 storm flaps

Double vents
at the back

Raglan sleeves

Straps to tighten
the wrists

Checked or
plain lining

Self belt with or
without belt loops

Double-breasted front

Vent

Beige/khaki   Dark blue   Black

Water-resistant cotton gabardine drill * Leather * Poplin

Jackets

Windbreaker

Lightweight windproof jacket, also called a windcheater.

Hood

Press buttons or a zip

Pockets

Rubber band
cuffed

Casual cut

Drawstrings

Elasticated hemline

Waterproof synthetics ∗ Nylon

Mackintosh

Pointed collar

Concealed fastening

Slant flap pockets

Straight silhouette

Casual cut

Mid-hip length

∗ Rubberised waterproof cotton ∗

Anorak

A waterproof, windproof pull-over jacket.

Hood

Drawstrings

No front opening (pull-over)

Kangaroo pocket

Simple square cut

Mid-hip length

Drawstrings or elastic bands at the cuffs

Waterproof, windproof materials Cotton ∗ Nylon

Bomber

A short, warm, waterproof jacket originally worn by pilots.

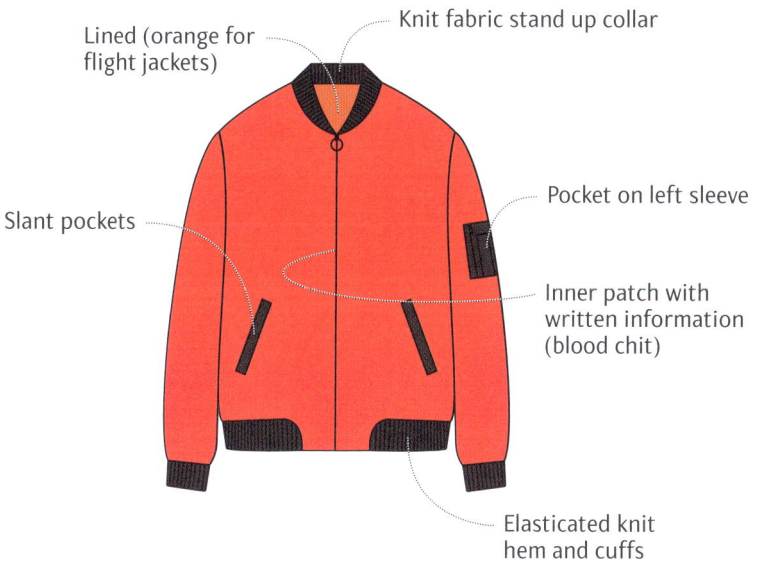

Lined (orange for flight jackets)

Knit fabric stand up collar

Slant pockets

Pocket on left sleeve

Inner patch with written information (blood chit)

Elasticated knit hem and cuffs

Cotton * Nylon

Mackinaw jacket

Originally a soldier's uniform made from blankets.

Usually red and black
shearling collar
buffalo check wool

Pointed or warm
shearling collar

4 front and
2 side pockets

Hip length

Button fastening

Wool ∗ Cotton ∗ Flannel ∗ Mackinaw cloth

Biker jacket

Inspired by leather jackets worn by US Air Force pilots.

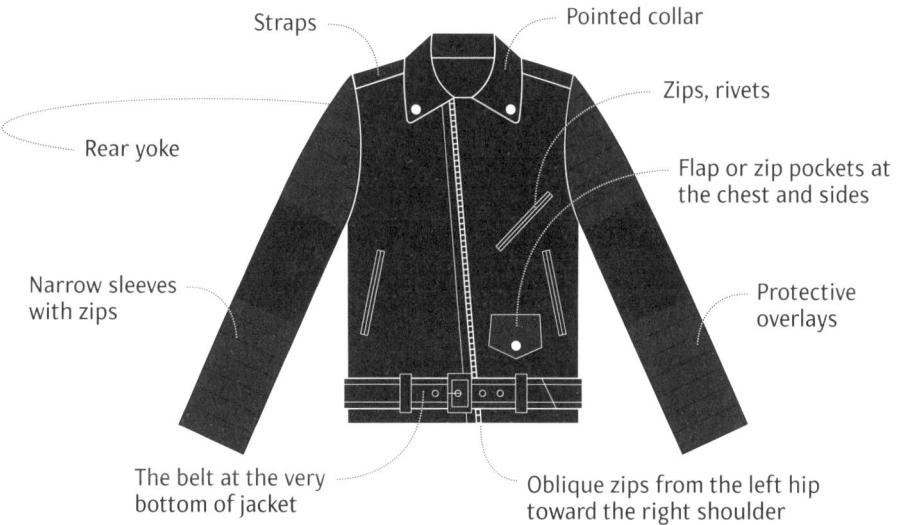

Straps

Pointed collar

Zips, rivets

Rear yoke

Flap or zip pockets at
the chest and sides

Narrow sleeves
with zips

Protective
overlays

The belt at the very
bottom of jacket

Oblique zips from the left hip
toward the right shoulder

* Leather *

M65 field jacket

Introduced in 1965 by the US Army.

Stand-up collar

Built-in hood, which can be rolled up and stowed in a special comparment on the collar

Shoulder straps

3 Zip fastening with press button flap

2 lower and 2 chest flap pockets

Khaki colour

Velcro wrists

Drawstrings to secure the hemline

Khaki

Dense, waterproof cotton sateen ∗ Cotton/polyester blends

Fishtail parka

Packable hood that can
be rolled into a special
compartment

Hood with or without
fur trim

3 Zip fastening with
a press button flap

Diagonal flap pockets

Drawstring at
the waist

Bifurcated 'fish 'tail'

Warm lining (wool,
quilted, etc.)

* Outer shell: cotton/nylon blend *
* Padding/fill - mohair or alpaca *

Denim jacket

Also called a jean jacket or trucker jacket.

Buttons

Yoke

Double seams

Lateral straps

Pointed collar

Flap patch pockets
with a button

Vertical single-welt
pockets

Unlined, or lined in
shearling or faux fur

Cuffs on the sleeves
and a lower hemline

∗ Denim ∗

Harrington jacket

Originally a lightweight golf jacket.

Check or tartan lining

Stand-up collar with
two button

Raglan sleeve

Zip fastening

Lateral pockets

Storm flap
on the back

Waterproof coating

Wide elastic band
along the cuffs
and hem

Lined with tartan or check fabric

Teflon-coated waterproof cotton ∗ Nylon ∗ Polyester ∗ Wool

Down jacket

Warm yet lightweight jacket with various details,
also called a puffer jacket.

Fur trim

With or without a hood

Waterproof,
windproof shell

Quilting and
padding

Pockets

Down or feather fill * Polyester wadding * Thinsulate™

Letterman
or varsity jacket

Jacket worn by student athletes in America.

Knick fabric stand-up collar · · · · · · · · · · · · · Quilted lining

University initial
on the chest

Press buttons

Contrast sleeves

Slant pockets

Hip length · · · · · · · · · · · · · Elasticated knit bands
at the cuffs and hem

Torso: boiled wool/Melton cloth ∗ Sleeves: leather or wool

79

Hoodie

Hooded sweatshirt that can be traced back
to Medieval monks' clothing.

Drawstring

Hood

Muff-style
pouch pocket

Cuffs

Zip fastener

Cotton knits ∗ Fleece

Fur coat

It came to symbolise status and wealth.
Details vary from one style to the next.

Fur on the outside

Shawl or lapel collar
in fur, with or without
lapels, or even no collar

Double-breasted
or single-breasted
front

With or without
cuffs, in fur

Fastens on the left or right
side with hooks, zips or
buttons, or can be belted

Natural fur * Faux fur

Mantle

A type of cloak from France.

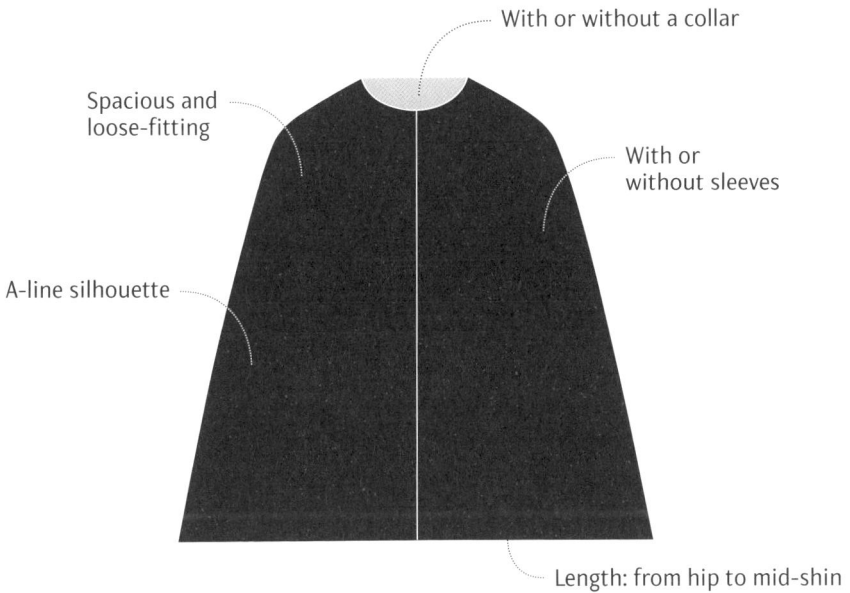

With or without a collar

Spacious and
loose-fitting

With or
without sleeves

A-line silhouette

Length: from hip to mid-shin

Wool * Broadcloth * Velvet * Satin * Fur

Shearling coat

A warm jacket made from pelts with the wool left on them,
or a synthetic version of the same.

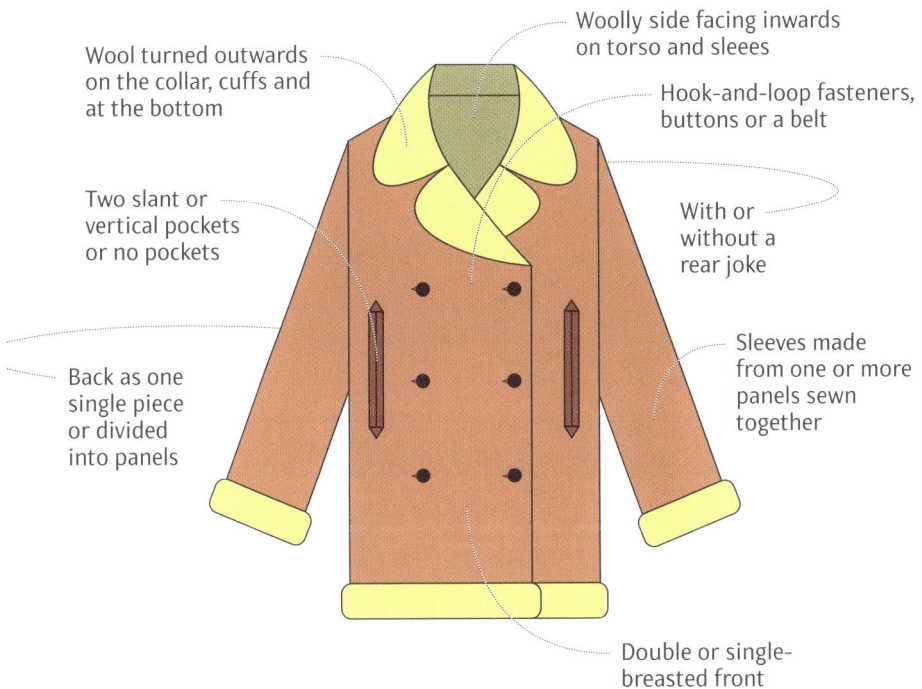

Wool turned outwards
on the collar, cuffs and
at the bottom

Woolly side facing inwards
on torso and sleees

Hook-and-loop fasteners,
buttons or a belt

Two slant or
vertical pockets
or no pockets

With or
without a
rear joke

Back as one
single piece
or divided
into panels

Sleeves made
from one or more
panels sewn
together

Double or single-
breasted front

Nappa leather * Karakul * Goatskin * Sheepskin
Merino * Enterfino shearling

Suit jacket

Flat or stand collar

Step pointed or shawl lapels

Chest pocket

Inner pocket

3–4 buttons on the cuffs

Vents: one central, two lateral, or none

Single-breasted (1-4 buttons) or double-breasted (2-6 buttons)

Wool ∗ Broadcloth ∗ Tweed ∗ Cady ∗ Cashmere Bouclé ∗ Cotton

Women´s jacket

Decorative elements and fittings, trim, fringe, etc.
Different materials.

Lapels

Semi-fitted silhouette

Pockets

Vent

Length; to waist
or mid-thigh

Bouclé * Tweed * Twill * Gabardine * Flannel
Wool * Cotton * Linen

Spencer

Short jacket with varied details.

Buttonholes or
buttons, toggles or
frog fasteners

Long sleeves

Fitted or boxy
silhouette

Wool ∗ Broadcloth ∗ Tweed ∗ Cady ∗ Cashmere ∗ Bouclé

Tailcoat

Men's evening coat for official events with a cutaway front.
Originally a part of the uniforms worn by
cavalry officers, called a coatee.

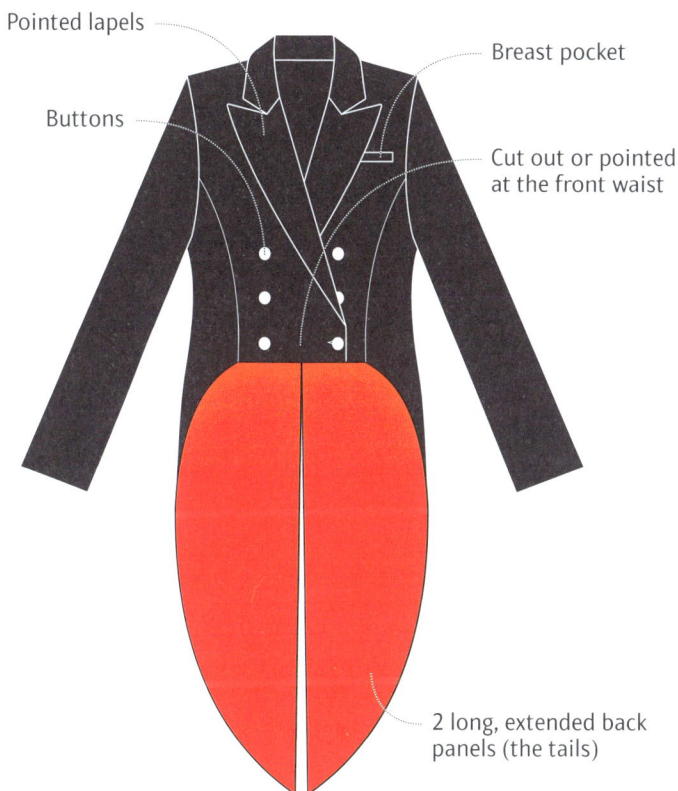

Pointed lapels

Breast pocket

Buttons

Cut out or pointed
at the front waist

2 long, extended back
panels (the tails)

Wool * Wool blends * Broadcloth * Cotton * Velvet * Silk

Smoking jacket

Called a tuxedo in the US, originally designed for tobacco smoking.

Step or shawl collar

Silk or satin lapels

Buttons covered
in fabric to
match the lapels

Pockets

Double or singled
breasted fold

2 vents or
none at all

Fine wool * Silk * Satin * Velvet * Jacquard

Blazer

Originally sports jacket worn to complement a casual dress code. Similar to a suit jacket, but more casual.

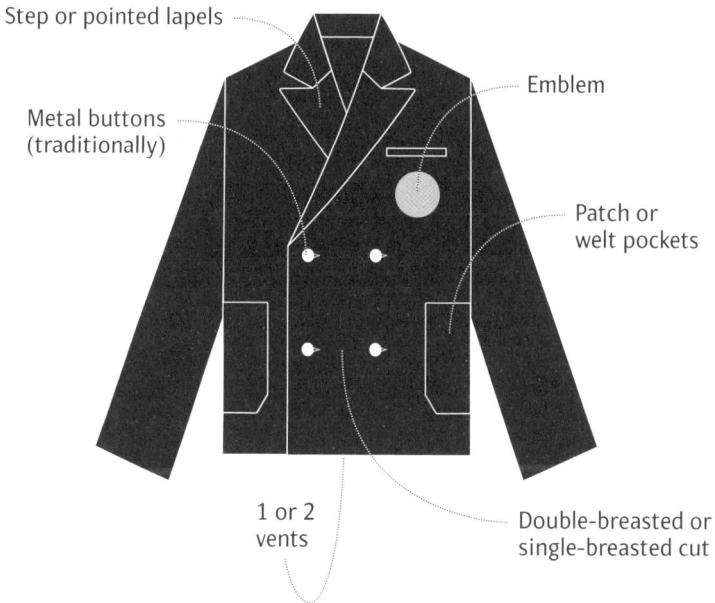

Step or pointed lapels

Emblem

Metal buttons (traditionally)

Patch or welt pockets

1 or 2 vents

Double-breasted or single-breasted cut

Linen * Cotton * Silk * Wool * Tweed * Flannel * Corduroy

Nehru jacket

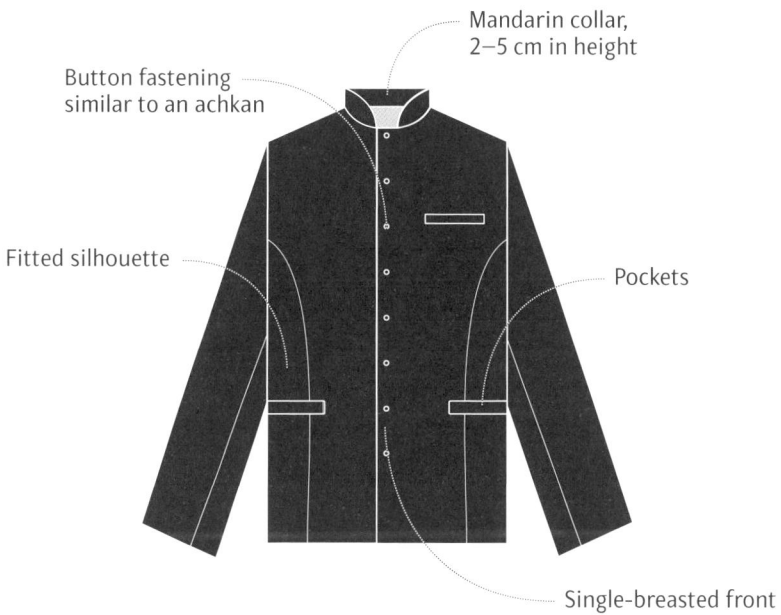

Mandarin collar,
2–5 cm in height

Button fastening
similar to an achkan

Fitted silhouette

Pockets

Single-breasted front

∗ Cotton ∗

Norfolk jacket

Originally a shooting coat popularised in the 1860s that was later used as golfing attire.

Classic lapels

2 vertical panels or fabric

3-4 wooden buttons

Matching belt

Protective patches

Box pleats on the rear shoulders

Deep rectangular pockets with flaps

Straight silhouette

Slits or vents

Single-breasted cut

Water-repellent check, striped or herringbone fabric
Wool * Corduroy * Twill * Leather * Suede * Tweed

Bolero

Originally an open short waistcoat worn by Spanish matadors.

With or without a collar

Open or with a clasp

Fitted V shape

Cropped to
the ribcage

Velvet * Satin * Cotton * Knits * Linen * Wool

Safari jacket

Originally a military uniform for warm weather conditions,
designed to protect from the sun.

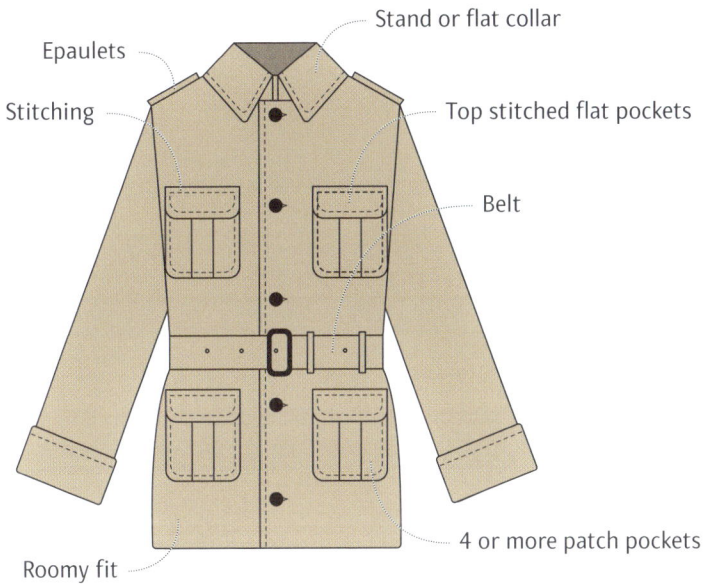

Epaulets

Stand or flat collar

Stitching

Top stitched flat pockets

Belt

4 or more patch pockets

Roomy fit

Earth tones

Khaki   Olive green   Beige   Sand   Brown

* Natural materials: cotton, linen *

Waistcoat

Originally part of three-piece suits.
Classic, sporty or trendy.

With or without a collar

Sleeveless

With or without
pockets

Single or
double-breasted
front

Denim * Wool * Cotton * Fleece * Fur
Leather * Satin * Corduroy

Shirts and Blouses

Button-front shirt

Menswear.
Worn loose over a T-shirt or tank top.

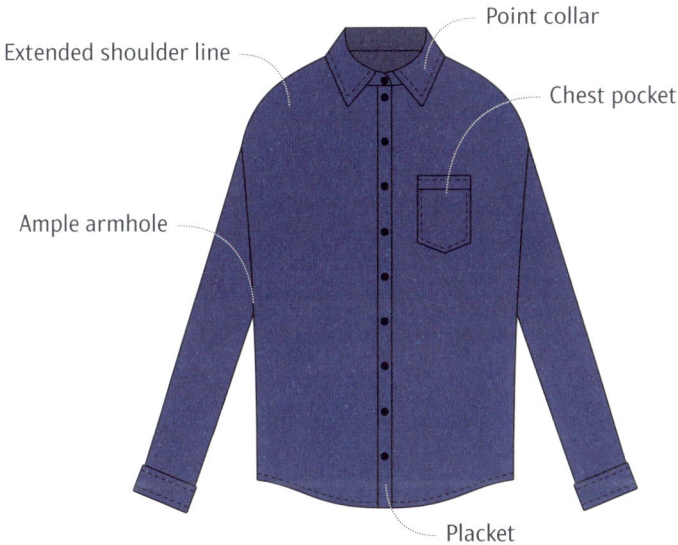

Point collar

Extended shoulder line

Chest pocket

Ample armhole

Placket

Jacquard * Flannel * Denim * Cotton * Poplin * Herringbone

Dress shirt

Menswear.

With or without a joke

Point collar

1 or 2 pockets with
or without flaps

Long, ¾ or
short sleeves

Centre packet with press
fasteners or buttons

Straight or
rounded hemline

Length: below mid-thigh

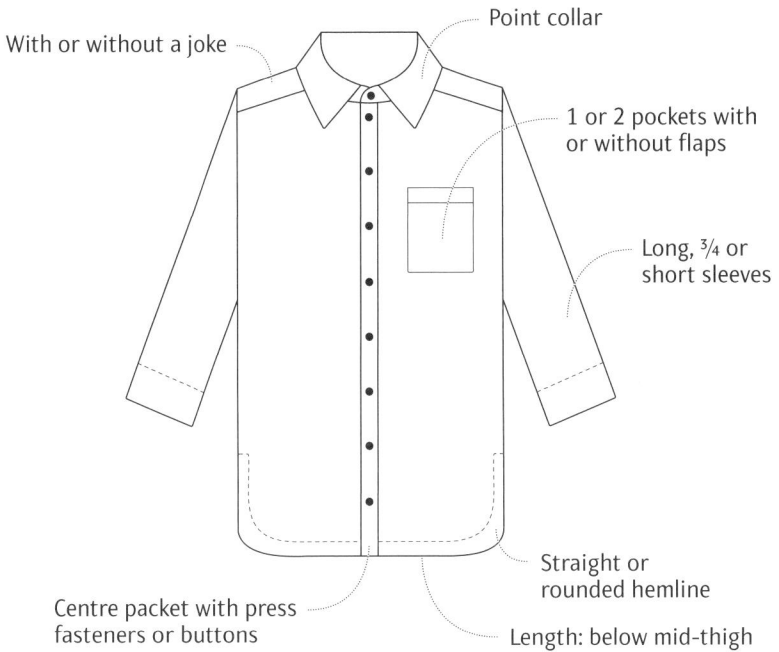

Cotton * Viscose * Poplin * Linen * Silk * Crepe * Sateen

Long sleeve T-shirt

Originally underwear.

Crew neck

Closed front made from
one piece of fabric

Nylon * Knits * Cotton * Viscose * Polyester

Marinière

Originally worn by seamen in the French navy. Also called *tricot rayé*. Defined by classic blue stripes, though other colours are often used today.

Horizontal stripes, originally white and blue

* Knits *

Polo neck

Also called a roll-neck or a turtleneck (USA, Canada).
Slim fit jumper with a high collar.

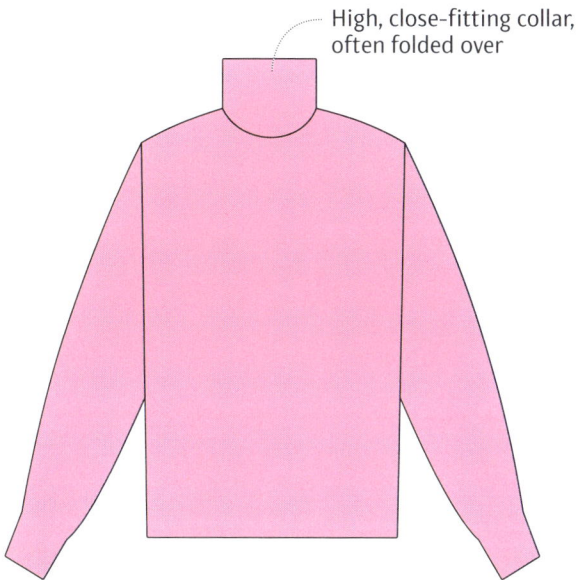

High, close-fitting collar,
often folded over

Jersey * Cashmere * Wool * Cotton * Knits * Silk

Jumper

Called a sweater in the USA. Various lengths, cuts and necklines.

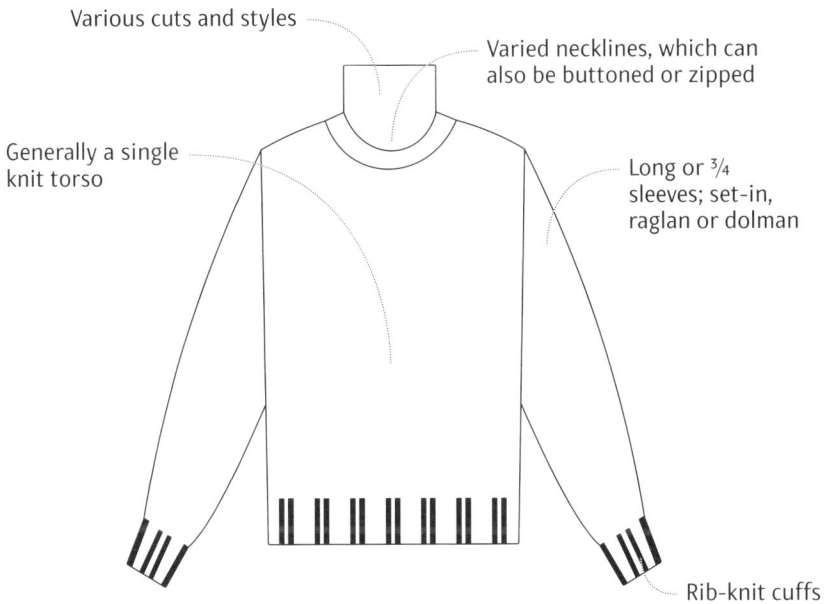

Various cuts and styles

Varied necklines, which can
also be buttoned or zipped

Generally a single
knit torso

Long or ¾
sleeves; set-in,
raglan or dolman

Rib-knit cuffs

Wool * Cotton * Acrylic * Cashmere * Mohair * Knits

Pullover

Originally sportswear for athletes Knit or crocheted.

Only opening is
a hole for the head,
no clasps or buttons.
Symmetrical or
asymmetrical cut, no
longer than 10 cm in
length

Rounded or square
necklines

Generally one panel
for the torso

Set-in or
raglan sleeves

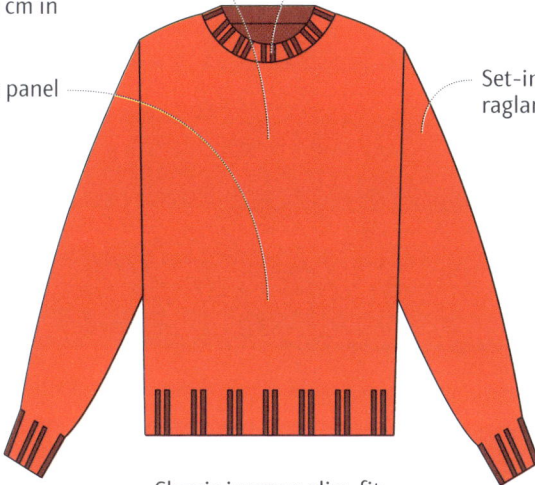

Classic jumper: slim-fit
with crew neck

Polo jumper with a point collar

Jumper dress

Wool * Cashmere * Cotton * Knits * Blended yarn

Sweatshirt

Originally clothing for sports.

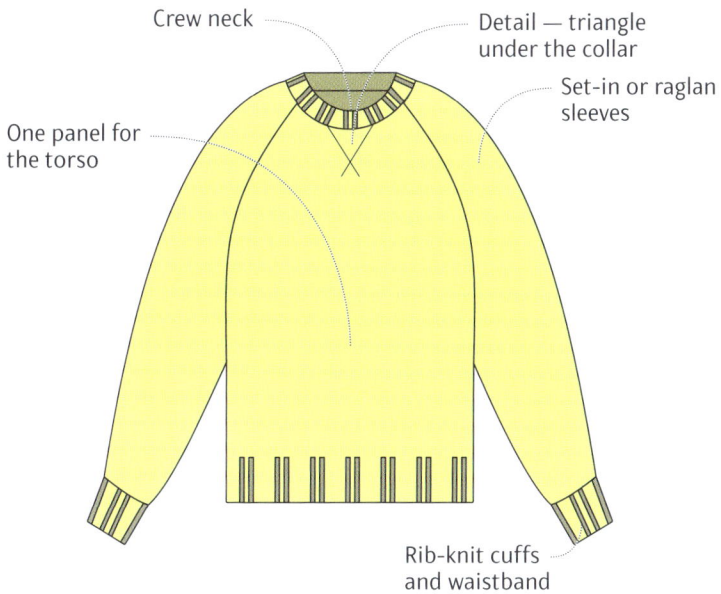

Crew neck

Detail — triangle
under the collar

Set-in or raglan
sleeves

One panel for
the torso

Rib-knit cuffs
and waistband

Cotton * Polyester * French terry * Fleece
Cashmere * Wool * Knits

V-neck pullover

Originally clothing for sports activities.

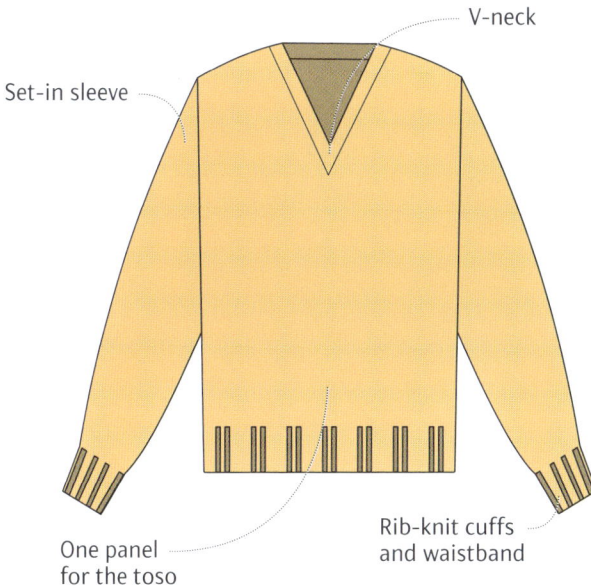

Set-in sleeve

V-neck

One panel
for the toso

Rib-knit cuffs
and waistband

Velvet * Satin * Cotton * Knits * Linen * Wool

Cardigan

Similar to a jumper, but with a front opening.

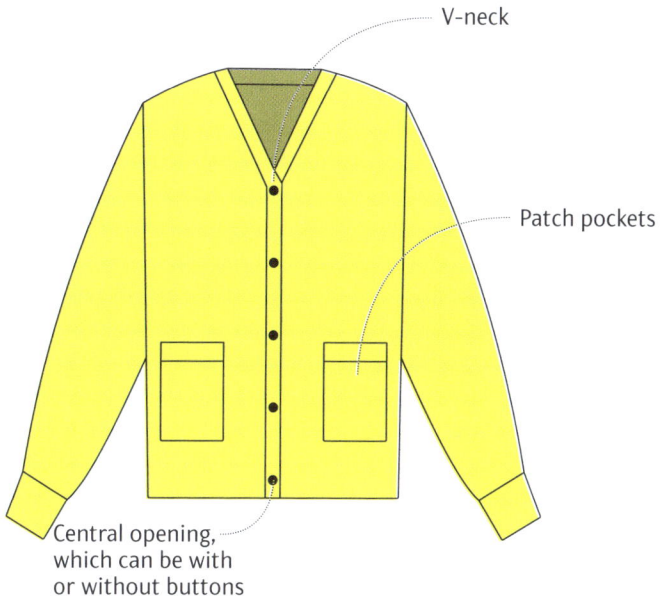

V-neck

Patch pockets

Central opening,
which can be with
or without buttons

Angora ✻ Viscose crepe ✻ Cotton ✻ Cashmere ✻ Mohair

Various tops and blouses

Fitted shirt button-up shirt

Sleeveless blouse

Body one-piece garment that covers the torso and crotch

Tunic Long, loose blouse with
or without a belt

Cossack high-neck tunic
with the fastening to
one side

Peplum top blouse with a gathered,
slightly flared strip of fabric
along the hemline

Shirt dress: a dress with
the cut and appearance
of a men's shirt

Tops and Dresses

Tunic dress

Simple, sack-shaped dress.

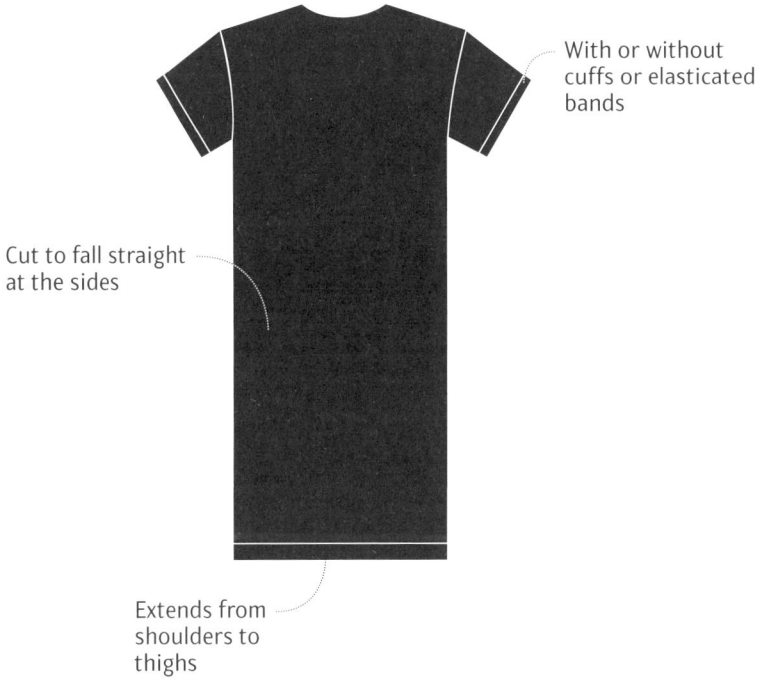

With or without
cuffs or elasticated
bands

Cut to fall straight
at the sides

Extends from
shoulders to
thighs

Silk * Viscose * Knits * Chiffon * Satin * Cotton

Polo shirt

The original sports uniform for polo.

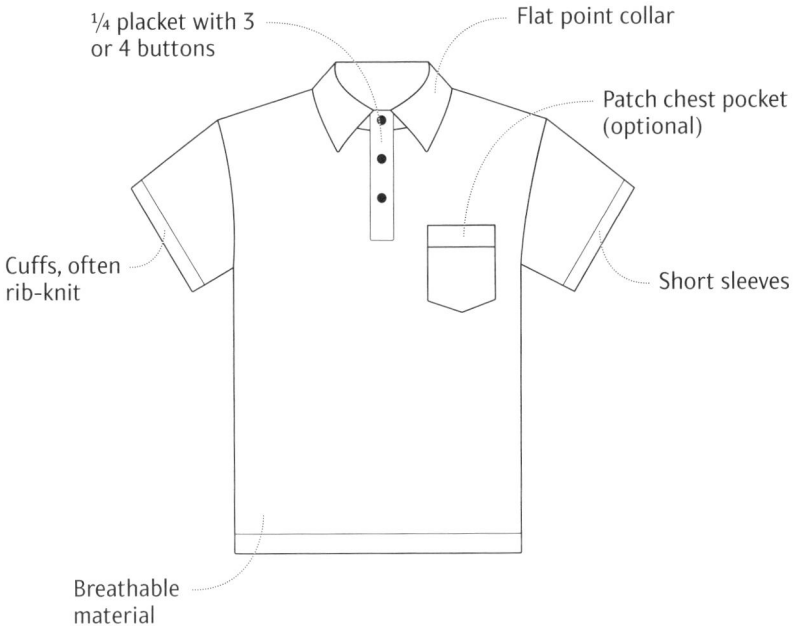

¼ placket with 3
or 4 buttons

Flat point collar

Patch chest pocket
(optional)

Cuffs, often
rib-knit

Short sleeves

Breathable
material

* Cotton pique *

T-shirt

Originally the underwear of the US infantry.

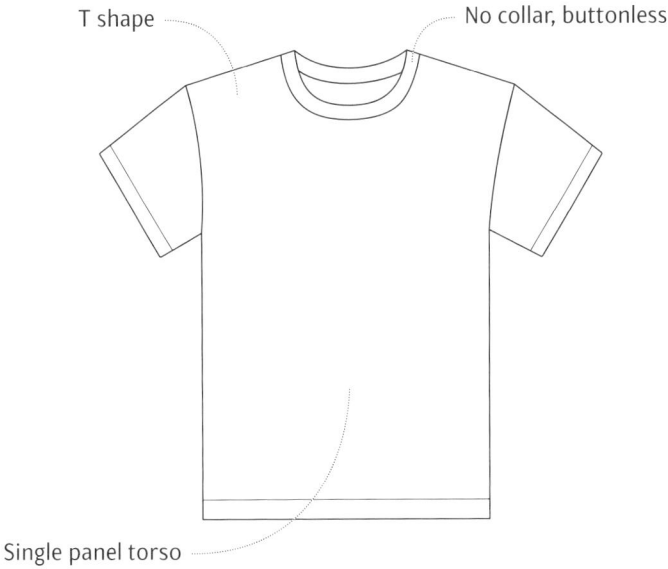

T shape ....

No collar, buttonless ....

Single panel torso ....

Polyester * Knits * Cotton * Viscose

Sleveless tops and vest

Halter Top

Open upper back, thin straps tie extend up and behind the neck

Vest or A-shirt

Rounded neckline, usually fitted to the body, often plain colour and with minimal decor

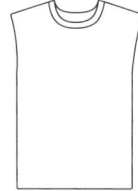

Sleveless shirt

T-shirt with no sleeves

Camisole

Sleveless top, with thin straps, often worn as an undergarment

Tube Top

A 'tube' of fabric with no straps and sleeves

Muscle Tank Top

Loose fitting sleeveless top, often worn to work out in

Racerback Top

Sleeveless top with straps that form a Y at the back

143

Crop top

Also called a half shirt, midriff top or cut-off shirt. Originally the top part of Indian saris (choli), though similar garments were part of traditional dress in Vietnam (yếm) and China (dudou).

Bandeau

A strip of fabric that covers the breasts. Similar to a strapless bra

Bra top

A top that takes the form of a bra

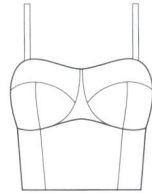

Bustier

Close-fitting garment
in the form of a
shortened corset or
basque

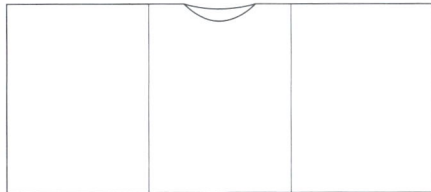

Kimono shirt

Loose fitting Japanese-inspired
garment whose construction is
defined by the large sleeves cut
as one with the torso

Polo dress

The dress version of the shirt worn by polo players.

¼ placket with
3 or 4 buttons

Flat point collar

Chest flap pocket
(optional)

Cuffs (often rib-knit)

Short sleeves

Breathable
material

* Cotton pique *

Sarafan

Jumper dress originally worn by Slavic women
over a shirt. Details and styles vary.

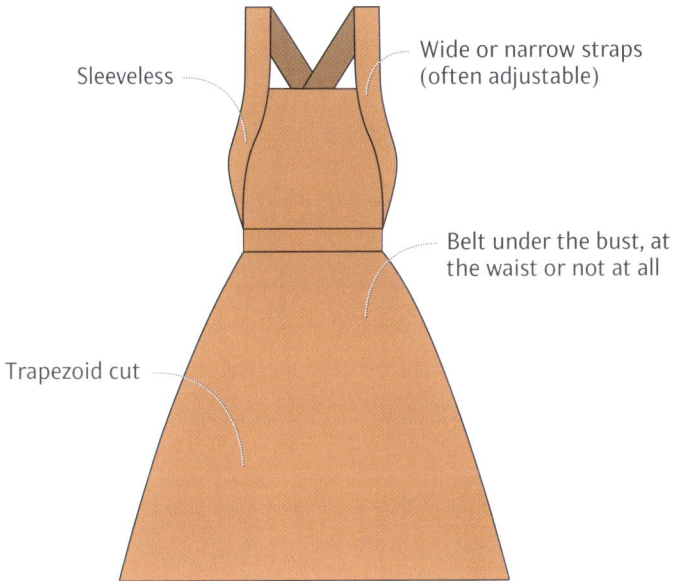

Sleeveless

Wide or narrow straps
(often adjustable)

Belt under the bust, at
the waist or not at all

Trapezoid cut

Cotton * Viscose * Batiste * Linen * Silk * Chiffon * Denim

Romper

Originally playwear for children. Details and styles vary.

Various necklines and collars

Straps, sleeves strapless

Shorts that are loose or tight-fitting

Cotton * Viscose * Linen * Silk * Denim
Corduroy * Velvet * Poplin

Princess dress

This style of dress, with a fitted torso
and A-line skirt, emerged in the Middle Ages.

Snug bodice

Natural low waistline

Decorative or simple

Large pieces of fabric

Full skirt

A-line silhouette

Silk * Taffeta * Chiffon * Gauze * Lace * Tulle * Satin

Little black dress

A black evening or cocktail dress that is usually
quite simple and without adornment.

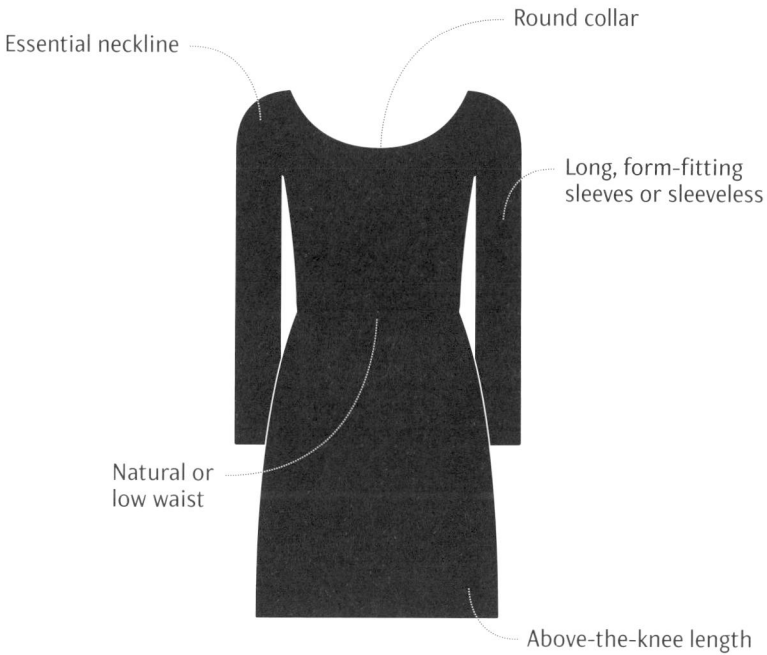

Essential neckline

Round collar

Long, form-fitting
sleeves or sleeveless

Natural or
low waist

Above-the-knee length

Cotton * Satin * Silk * Jersey * Knits * Viscose

Babydoll dress

Short dress with a full hemline.

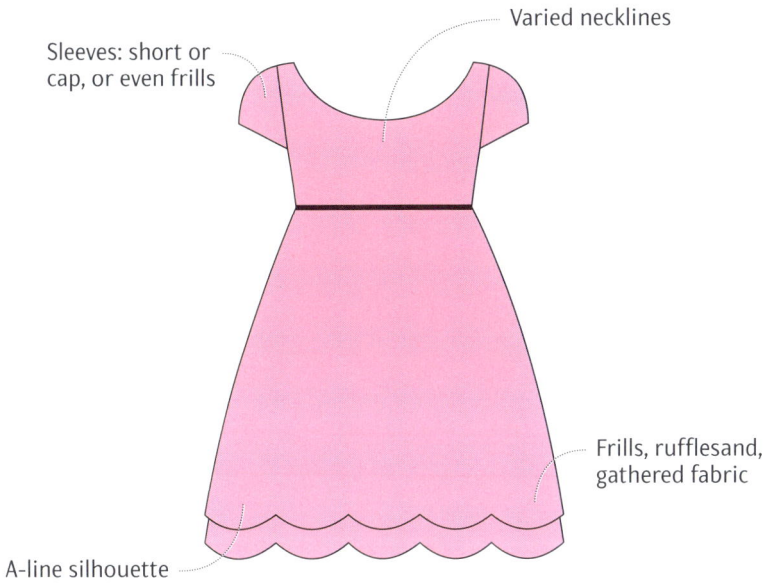

Sleeves: short or
cap, or even frills

Varied necklines

Frills, rufflesand,
gathered fabric

A-line silhouette

Silk * Batiste * Chiffon * Lace * Gauze * Organza * Crepe

Mermaid dress

Similar to a trumped dress. Fitted at the torso,
hips and thighs to widen at the knee.

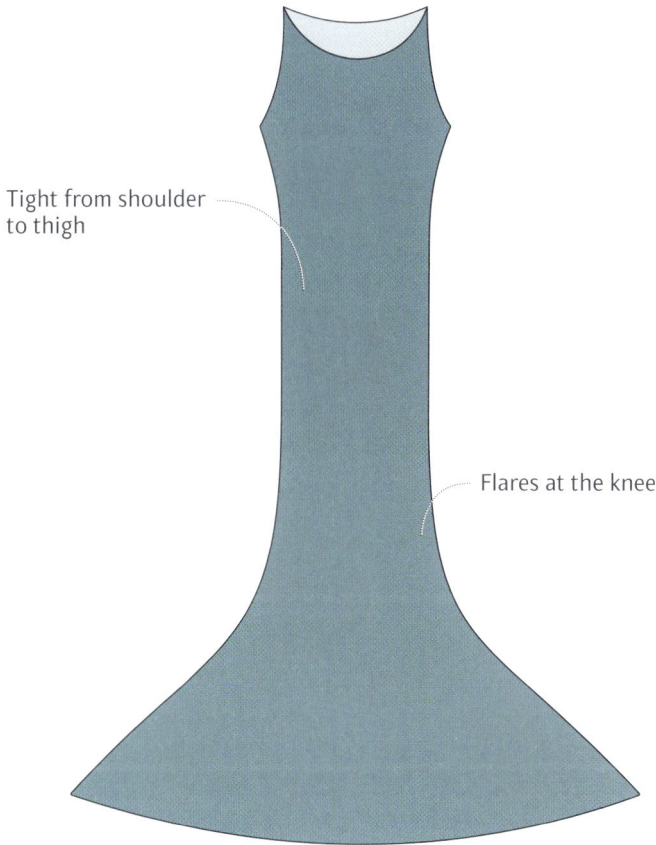

Tight from shoulder
to thigh

Flares at the knee

Satin * Silk * Taffeta * Chiffon * Gauze * Lace * Tulle

Sack dress

Styles and details vary.

With or without
sleeves

Loose free-flowing
silhouette

Ovoid cut that tapers
at the bottom

Cotton * Viscose * Jersey * Jacquard * Taffeta * Wool

Empire dress

A high-waisted dress, gathered just below the bust
with a long, loose skirt which skims the body

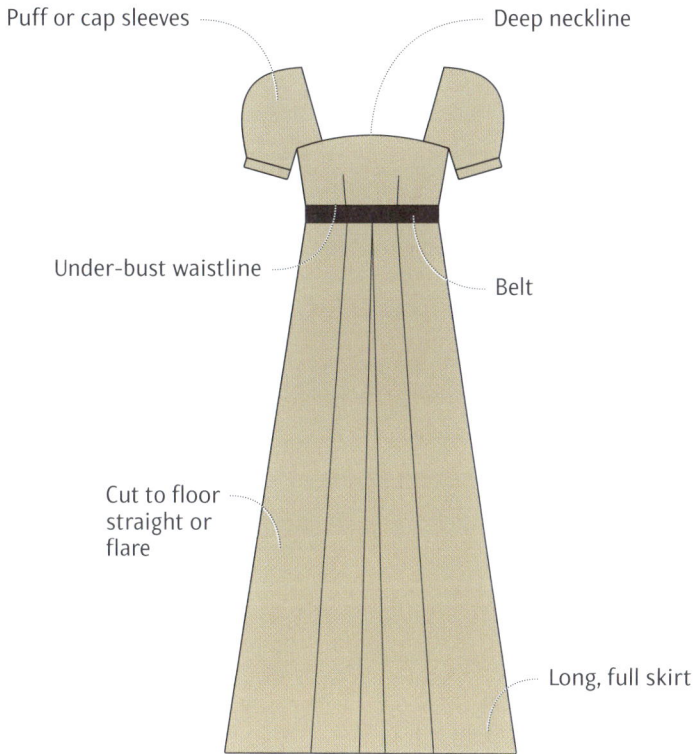

Puff or cap sleeves .... Deep neckline

Under-bust waistline ....

.... Belt

Cut to floor
straight or
flare ....

.... Long, full skirt

Batiste * Satin * Muslin * Crepe * Wool * Tulle * Taffeta

Shirt dress

Knee-length shirt.

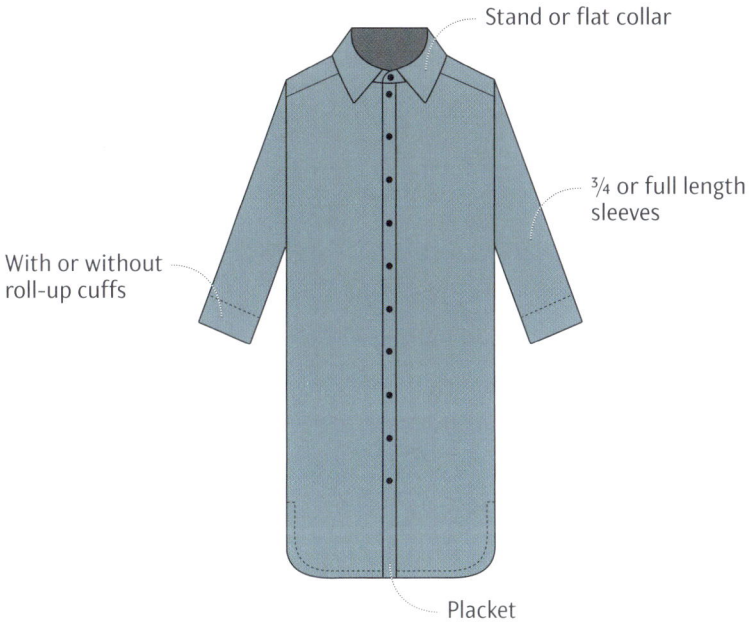

Stand or flat collar

¾ or full length sleeves

With or without roll-up cuffs

Placket

Viscose * Linen * Silk * Denim * Corduroy * Poplin * Cotton

Sheath dress

A slim, feminine figure-enhancing dress. Styles and details vary, though generally with short sleeves and a knee-length cut.

Round neckline

Sleeveless or
off-shoulder

Knee to floor length

Cotton * Satin * Silk * Jersey * Knits * Viscose

Kimono

Traditional Japanese clothing.

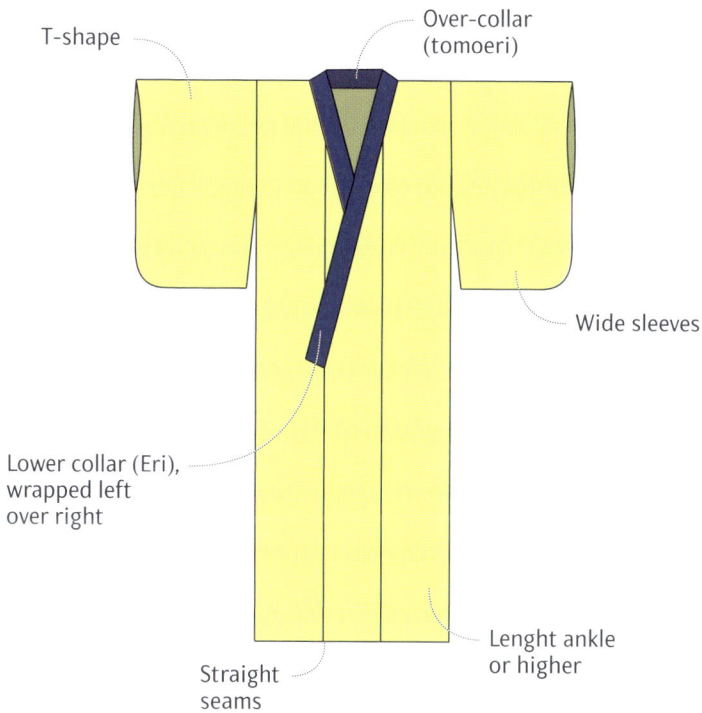

T-shape

Over-collar
(tomoeri)

Wide sleeves

Lower collar (Eri),
wrapped left
over right

Lenght ankle
or higher

Straight
seams

Polyester * Silk * Silk-crepe * Sateen * Crepe Back Satin

Bubble dress

Defined by a round, voluminous skirt held in place
by inner draping. Styles and details vary.

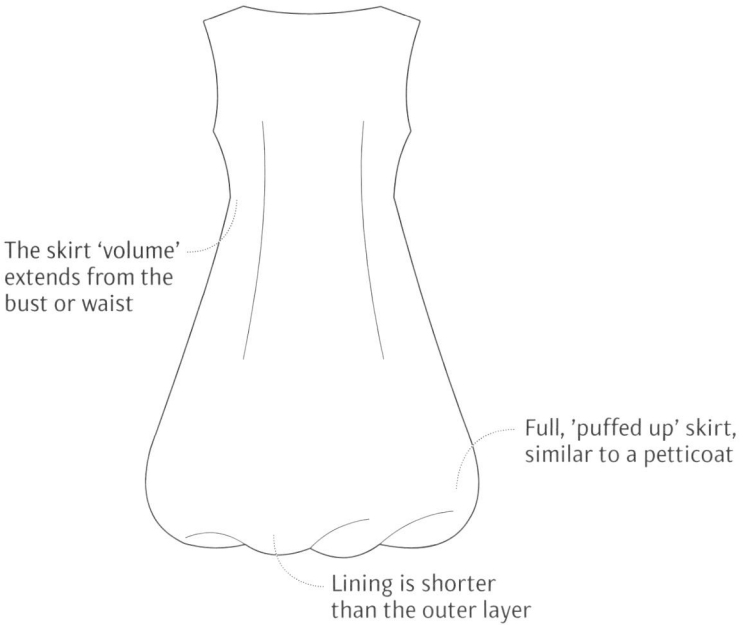

The skirt 'volume'
extends from the
bust or waist

Full, 'puffed up' skirt,
similar to a petticoat

Lining is shorter
than the outer layer

Satin ∗ Organza ∗ Taffeta ∗ Tulle ∗ Jacquard ∗ Crepe ∗ Viscose

Slip dress

Nightgown turned dress.

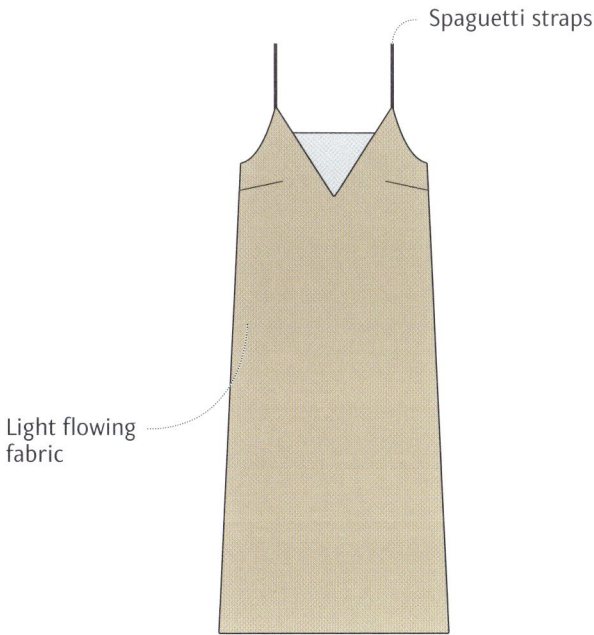

Spaguetti straps

Light flowing
fabric

Crepe * Lace * Satin * Silk * Velvet * Chiffon

Tier dress

Long or short, defined by 'tiers' made of ruffles.
Styles and details vary.

Ruffle 'tiers'

Empire
waistline

Creates and A-line

Cotton * Viscose * Jacquard * Taffeta * Silk * Chiffon

Tank dress

Straight silhouette dress.

Neckline: square, oval, scoop or V-shaped

* Knits *

Grecian maxi dress

Inspired by the national clothing of Greece: the peplos and chiton.

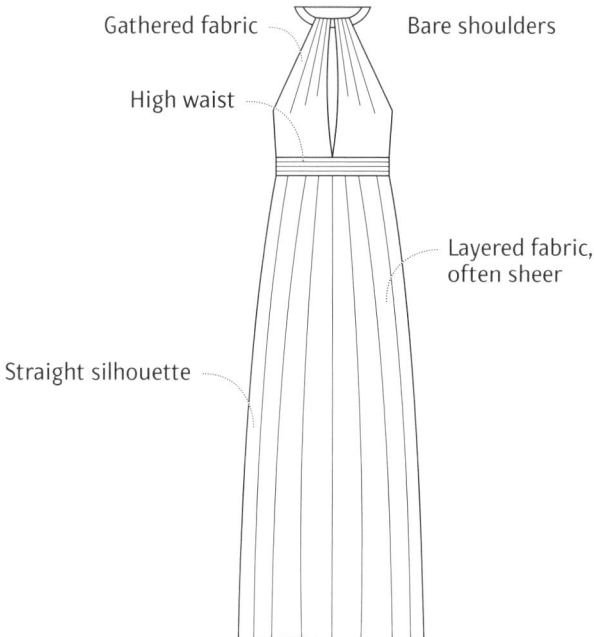

Gathered fabric

Bare shoulders

High waist

Layered fabric, often sheer

Straight silhouette

Cotton * Viscose * Silk * Chiffon * Linen * Crepe * Gauze

Sari dress

Inspired by Hindu women's garments from India. A single piece of fabric is wrapped around the body, the outer end of which is draped over the left shoulder. Styles and details vary.

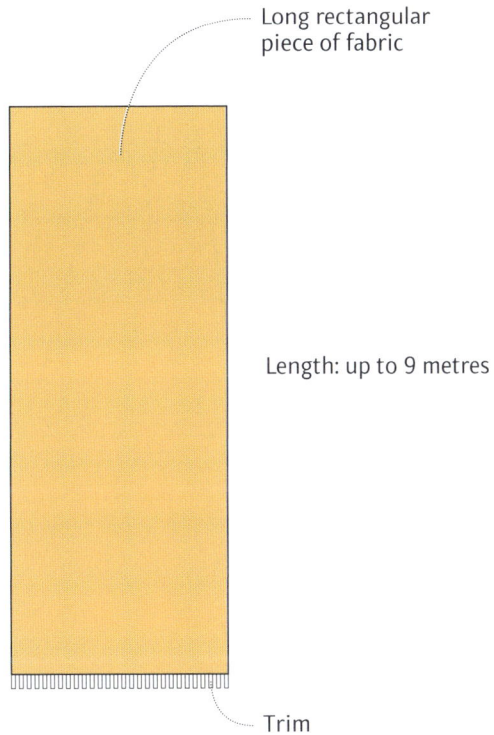

Long rectangular
piece of fabric

Length: up to 9 metres

Trim

Georgette * Crepe * Chiffon * Organza * Cotton * Silk * Gauze

New Look dress

Snug bodice

Narrow rounded shoulders

Sleeves: ¾ length, short or cap, or even frills

Waistline raised above the natural waistline by 3-5 cm

Hourglass silhouette

Full A-line skirt

Below-the-knee length

Cotton * Viscose * Jacquard * Taffeta * Silk * Chiffon

Denim dress

Yoke

Point collar

Chest pockets

Buttons

Cuffed sleeves

Patch or slash pockets
for the hands

Double topstitching

Placket

* Denim *

Qipao dress

Form-fitting dress from China, also known as a cheongsam.

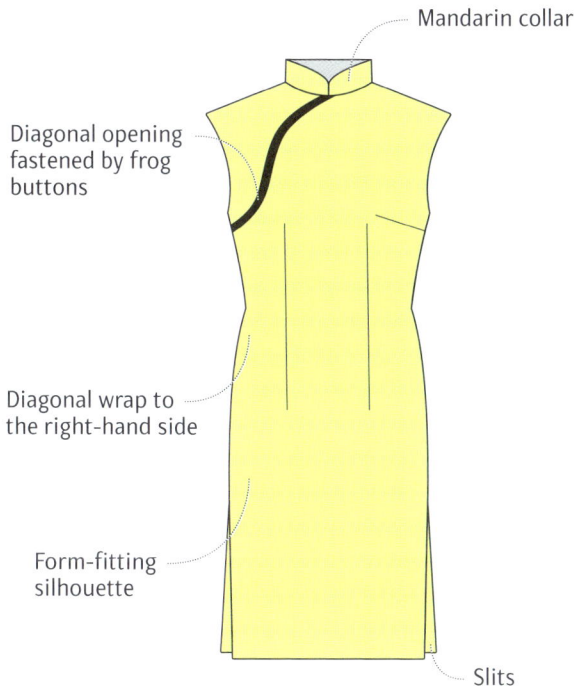

Mandarin collar

Diagonal opening
fastened by frog
buttons

Diagonal wrap to
the right-hand side

Form-fitting
silhouette

Slits

∗ Silk Satin ∗

Wrap dress

Styles and details vary.

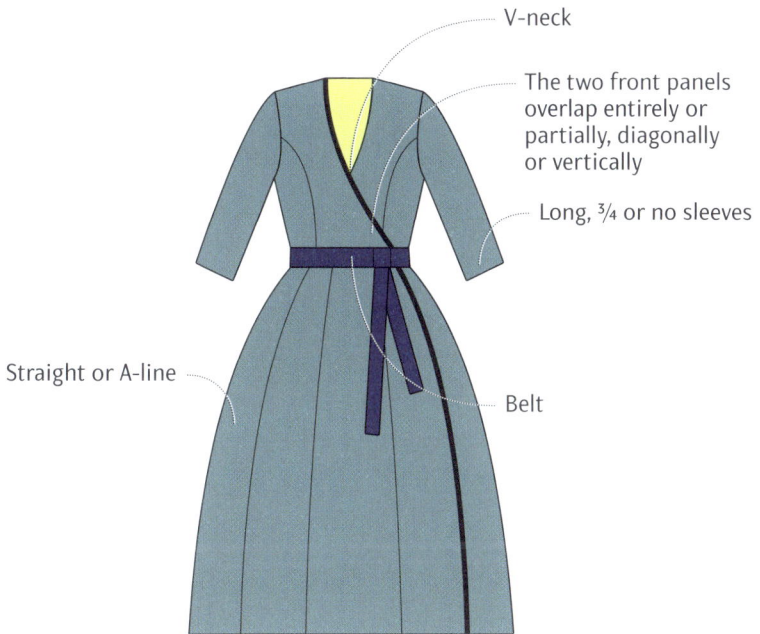

V-neck

The two front panels overlap entirely or partially, diagonally or vertically

Long, ¾ or no sleeves

Straight or A-line

Belt

Poplin * Linen * Cotton * Jersey * Viscose * Silk

Trousers
and Shorts

Classic tailored trousers

Straight-leg trousers with creases and/or cuffs.

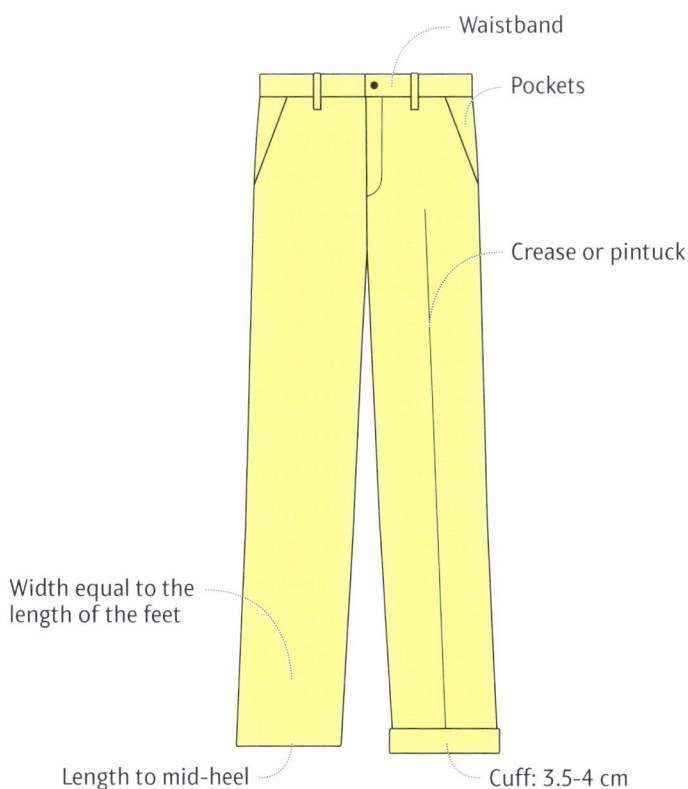

Waistband

Pockets

Crease or pintuck

Width equal to the
length of the feet

Length to mid-heel

Cuff: 3.5-4 cm

Smooth wool * Tweed * Blended fabrics

Shorts

Shorts trousers.

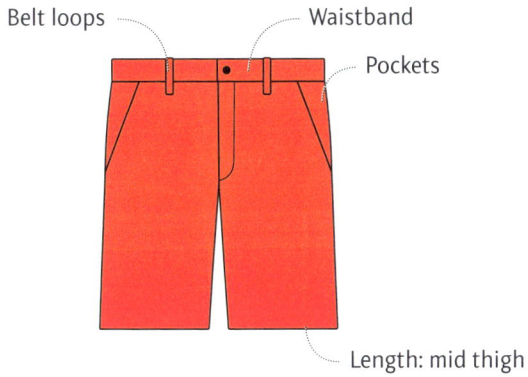

Belt loops · · · · · · · · · · · Waistband

Pockets

Length: mid thigh

Cotton * Denim * Knits * Velvet * Wool * Suiting Fabric
Leather * Synthetic materials

Hot pants

Short shorts.

Belt loops .... Waistband

Pockets

To the lower
buttocks

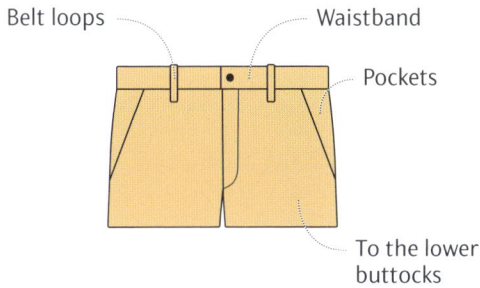

Cotton * Denim * Knits * Velvet * Wool * Suiting fabric
Leather * Synthetic materials

Cropped trousers

Trousers cut to a length that is anywhere
between the knee and just above the ankle.

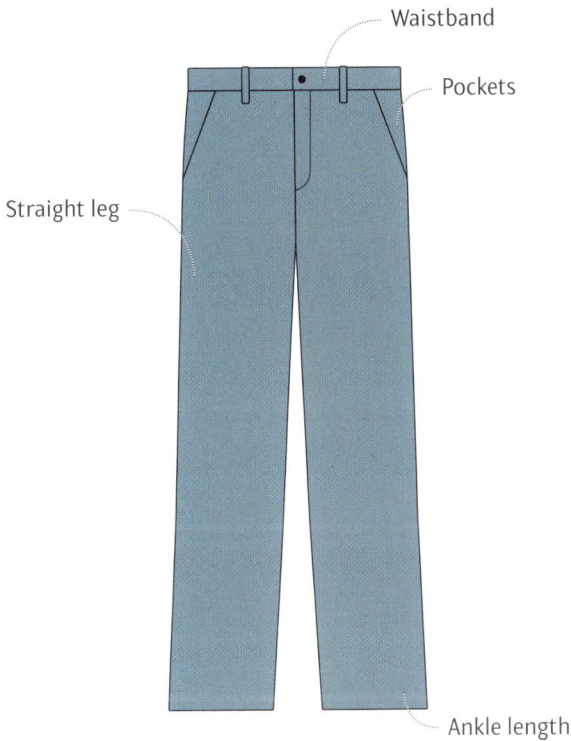

Waistband

Pockets

Straight leg

Ankle length

Wool ∗ Tweed ∗ Linen ∗ Blended fabrics ∗ Cotton

Stirrup leggings

Originally used as jodhpurs for male equestrians.

Details and styles
vary, though
generally snug-fitting

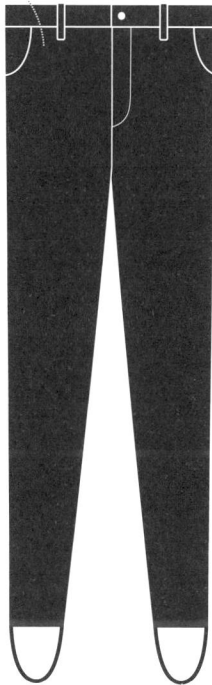

A strap, called a stirrup,
extends under the foot to
hold the trousers in place

Wool * Knits

Barrel leg trousers

Darted high waist trousers that are wider at the hips
and leg to then taper at the ankle.

High waist

Darts to shape
the waist

Wide in the hips

Tapered leg

Denim * Leather * Satin * Linen * Silk
Brocade * Knits * Cotton

Cigarette trousers

Slim fit trousers with straight, very narrow legs.

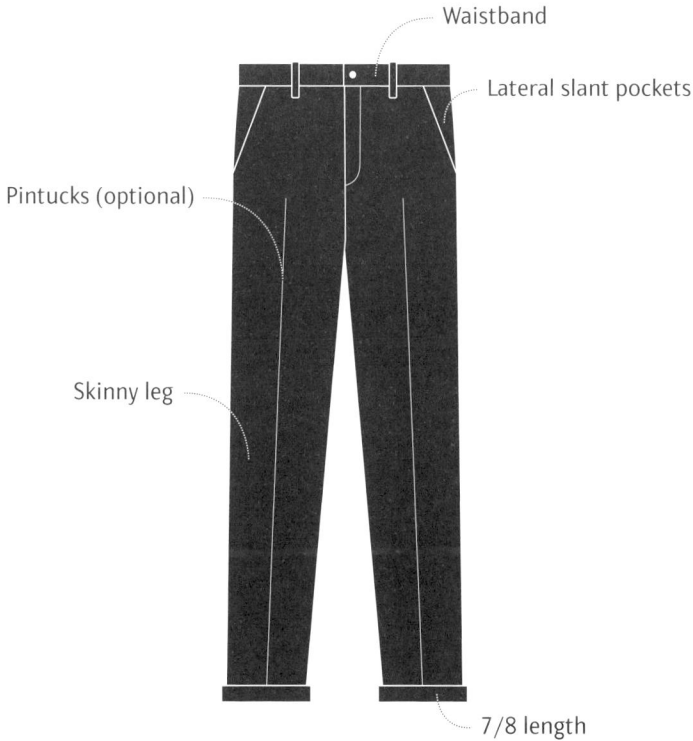

Waistband

Lateral slant pockets

Pintucks (optional)

Skinny leg

7/8 length

Denim * Satin * Corduroy * Silk * Fine wool * Dense cotton

Palazzo trousers

Long trousers cut with a loose, extremely wide leg
that flares out from the waist.

High waist

Extra-wide leg

Wool blends ∗ Satin ∗ Chiffon ∗ Knits ∗ Denim ∗ Linen
Cashmere ∗ Tweed ∗ Leather ∗ Cotton

Gauchos

Originally the loose-fitting trousers of South American cowboys.

Wide waistband

Flared from the hip

Mid-calf or ankle length

Wool ∗ Leather ∗ Suede ∗ Chiffon ∗ Silk ∗ Cotton

Hakama

Originally traditional samurai wear. For men, they are
fastened at the hips; for women, at the waist.

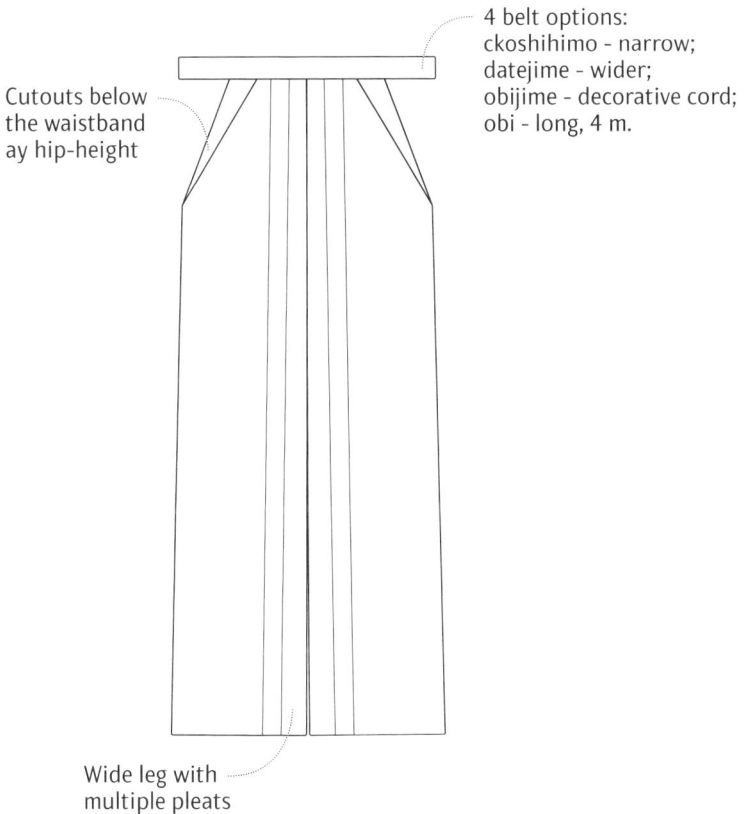

4 belt options:
ckoshihimo - narrow;
datejime - wider;
obijime - decorative cord;
obi - long, 4 m.

Cutouts below
the waistband
ay hip-height

Wide leg with
multiple pleats

Stiff silk * Dense cotton * Linen * Blended fabrics

Pyjama trousers

Originally the 'uniform' of men and women in India, these loose-fitting trousers were brought to the UK as men's loungewear.

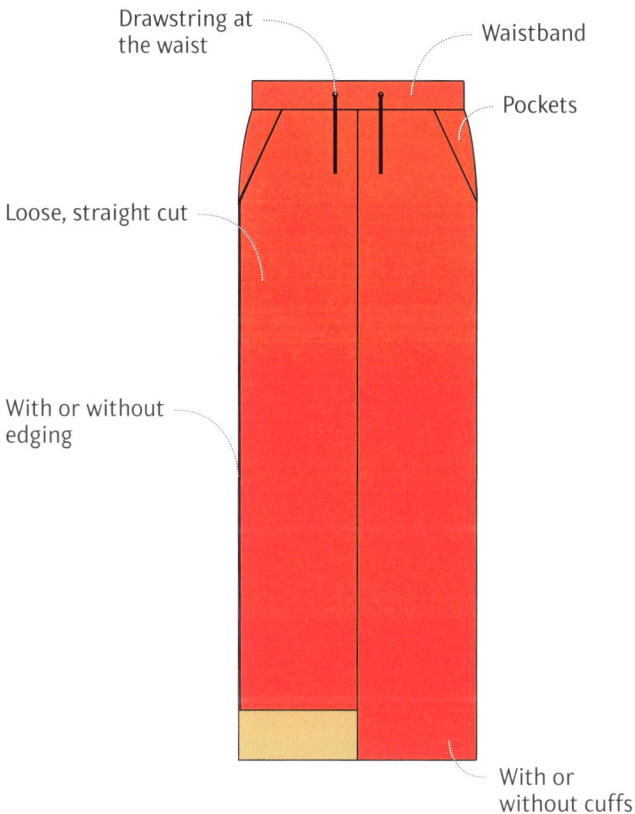

Drawstring at the waist

Waistband

Pockets

Loose, straight cut

With or without edging

With or without cuffs

Cotton ✳ Silk ✳ Satin ✳ Batiste

213

Capris

Cropped trousers, perfect for the beach.

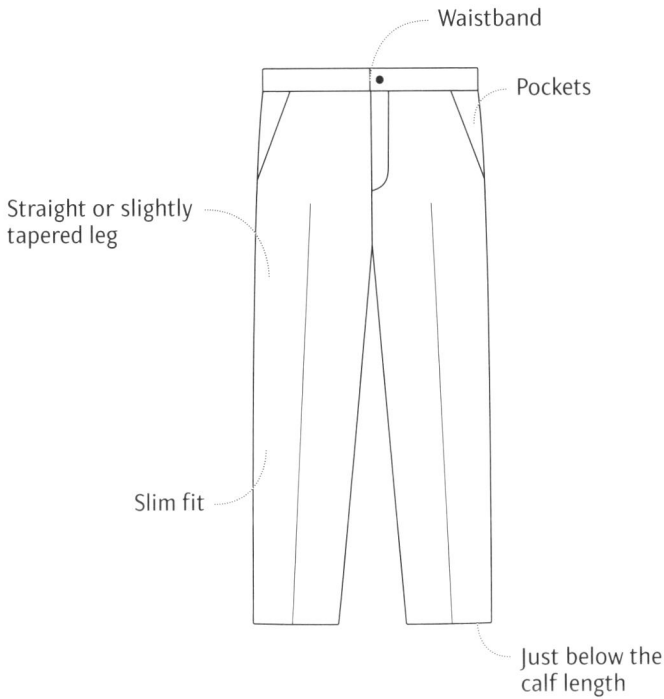

Waistband

Pockets

Straight or slightly
tapered leg

Slim fit

Just below the
calf length

Wool * Denim * Cotton

Bermuda shorts

Originally part of the uniform worn
by British soldiers in the colonies.

Similar to classic trousers
with belt loops

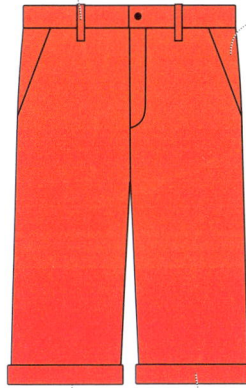

Pockets

Leg cut to just
above the knee

Cuffs: 2—5 cm

Linen * Viscose * Blended fabrics * Denim * Cotton

Joggers

Casual trousers made for jogging.

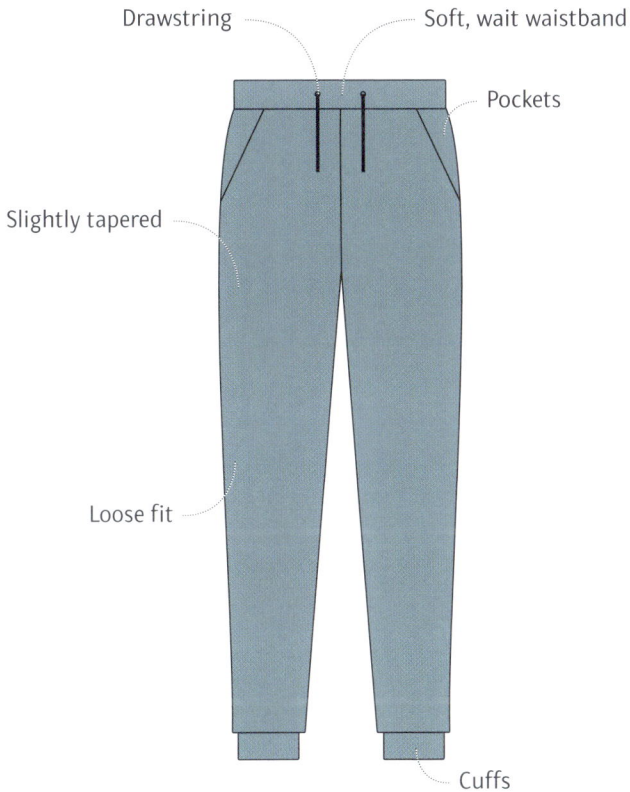

Drawstring

Soft, wait waistband

Pockets

Slightly tapered

Loose fit

Cuffs

Linen ∗ Knits ∗ French terry ∗ Dense cotton

Flares

Also called bell bottoms, these trousers were
once worn by American sailors.

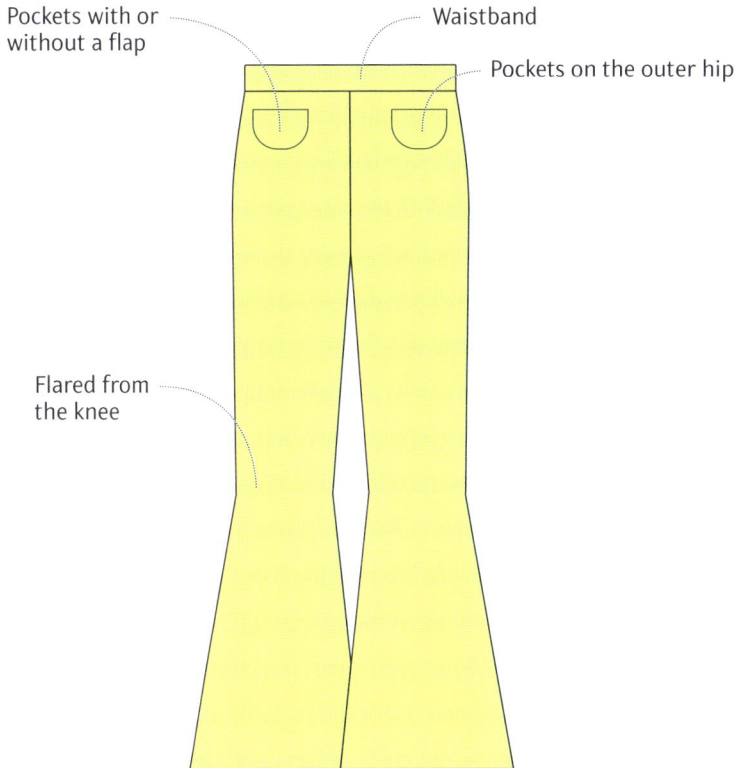

Pockets with or
without a flap

Waistband

Pockets on the outer hip

Flared from
the knee

Wool * Denim * Cotton

Split skirt

Wide-leg trousers that look like a skirt.

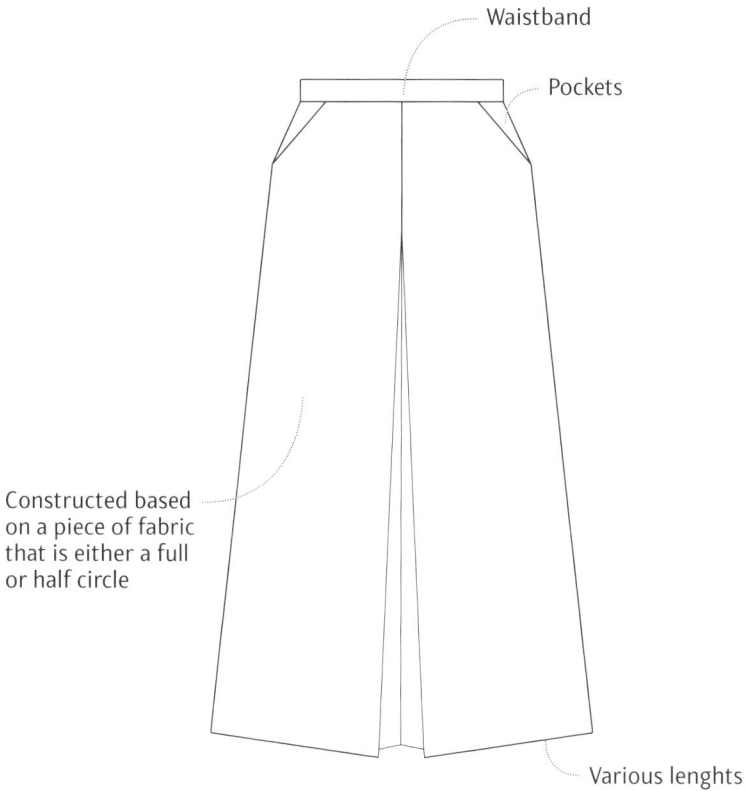

Waistband

Pockets

Constructed based
on a piece of fabric
that is either a full
or half circle

Various lenghts

Silk * Chiffon * Crepe de Chine * Knits

Cargo trouser

Practical trousers originally worn by the British Armed Forces.

Waistband

Pockets

Wide baggy cut

One or more additional
patch pockets

Reinforcements
on the knees

✳ Used-look cotton fabric ✳

Riding breeches

Originally tight-fitting, hard-wearing woollen riding trousers,
they often were constructed to avoid seams on the inner leg.

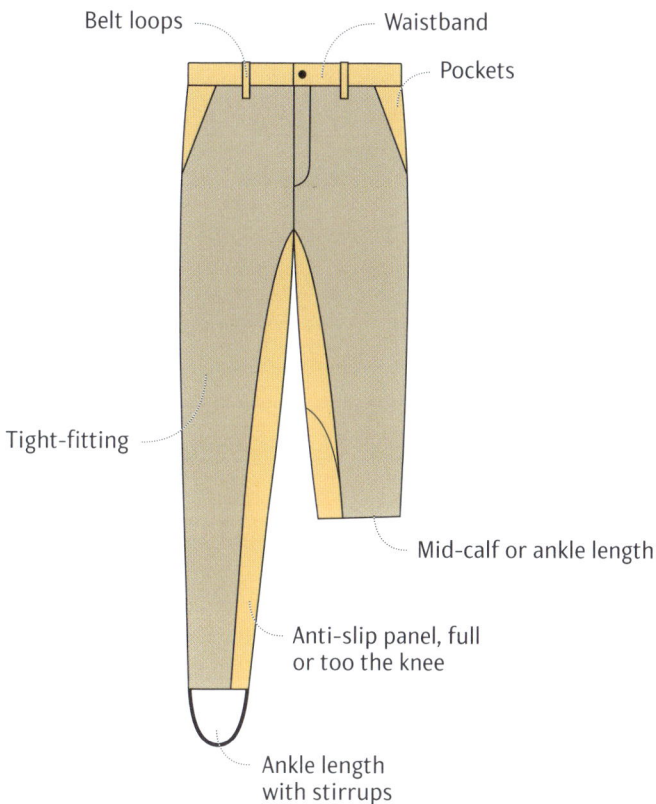

Belt loops

Waistband

Pockets

Tight-fitting

Mid-calf or ankle length

Anti-slip panel, full
or too the knee

Ankle length
with stirrups

Wool * Leather * Suede

Breeches

Trousers reaching to or just below the knees
and often tapered to fit closely.

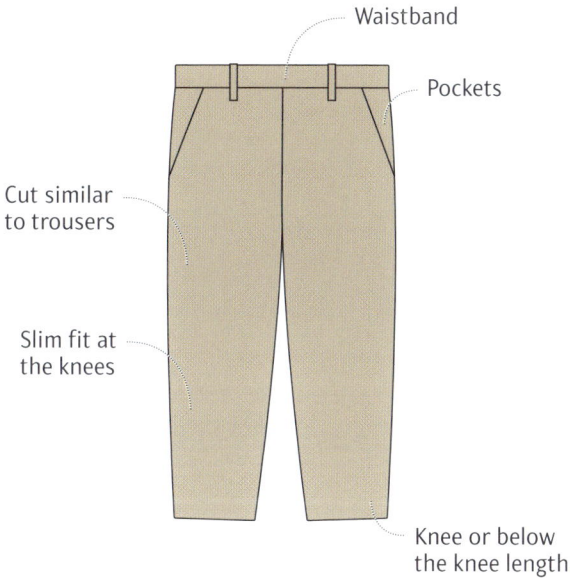

Waistband

Pockets

Cut similar
to trousers

Slim fit at
the knees

Knee or below
the knee length

Sateen * Satin * Corduroy * Denim * Leather * Cotton

Jodhpurs

Adapted from an ancient Indian style of trouser, jodhpurs fit snug at the calf but are flared for a loose fit at the upper thigh and hips. They are similar in cut to Gallifet trousers.

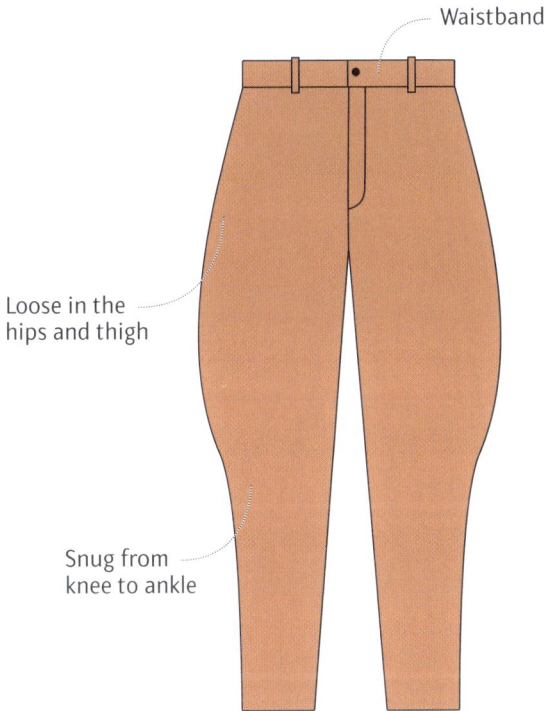

Waistband

Loose in the
hips and thigh

Snug from
knee to ankle

Wool * Tweed * Silk * Satin * Denim * Cotton

Culottes

Originally worn for riding and cycling.
A hybrid of wide trousers and a skirt.

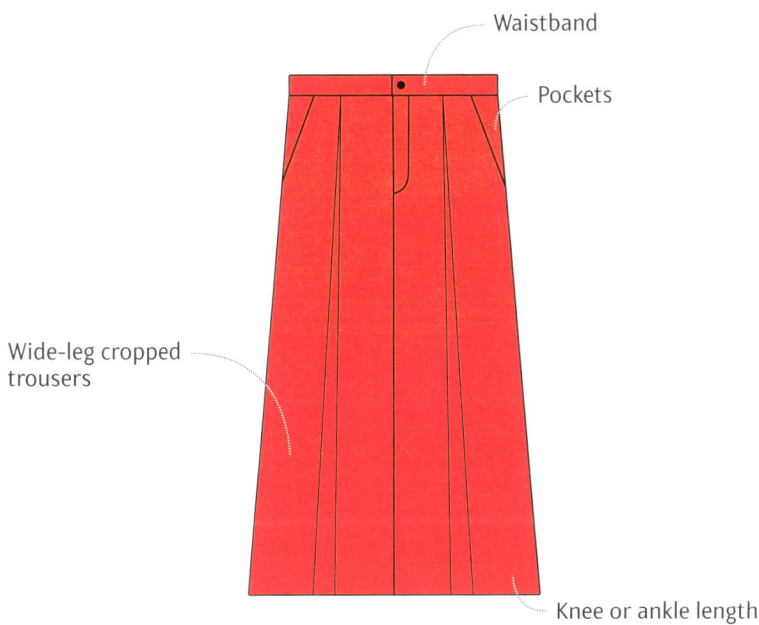

Waistband

Pockets

Wide-leg cropped
trousers

Knee or ankle length

Wool ∗ Silk ∗ Denim ∗ Corduroy ∗ Tweed
Jacquard Moire ∗ Velvet ∗ Dense cotton

233

Cycling shorts

Also known as bike shorts, they were originally worn when cycling to reduce wind resistance, wick sweat from the skin, and protect from friction.

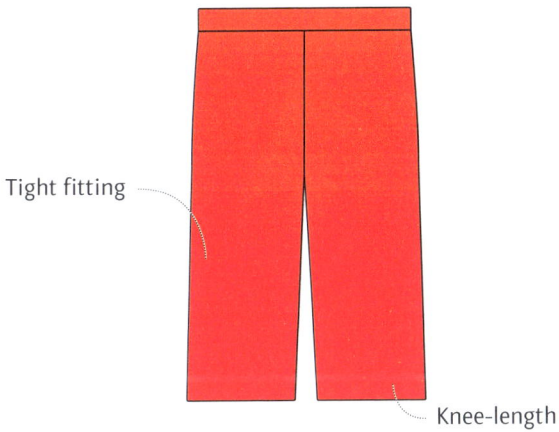

Tight fitting

Knee-length

* Polyamide and elastane blends *

Jeans

Originally work trousers made of hemp canvas.

Belt loops

Waistband

Metal rivets

Pockets

Fly

Double stitching

Indigo

* Denim *

Boyfriend jeans

Baggy jeans often with a used-look wash. Denim free
from elastane for an authentic fit.

Special rise
for women

Classic 5-pocket cut

Straight leg

Fly flap, as in the
classic jeans

Rips distressed details

Stitching

Rolled cuffs

* Denim *

239

Mum jeans

High-waisted jeans that were fashionable
in the 1980s and early 1990s.

Buttons

High waist

Waistband

Pockets

Looser in
the hips

Stitching

Rolled cuffs

* Dense denim *

Harem trousers

The national trousers of the Middle East.

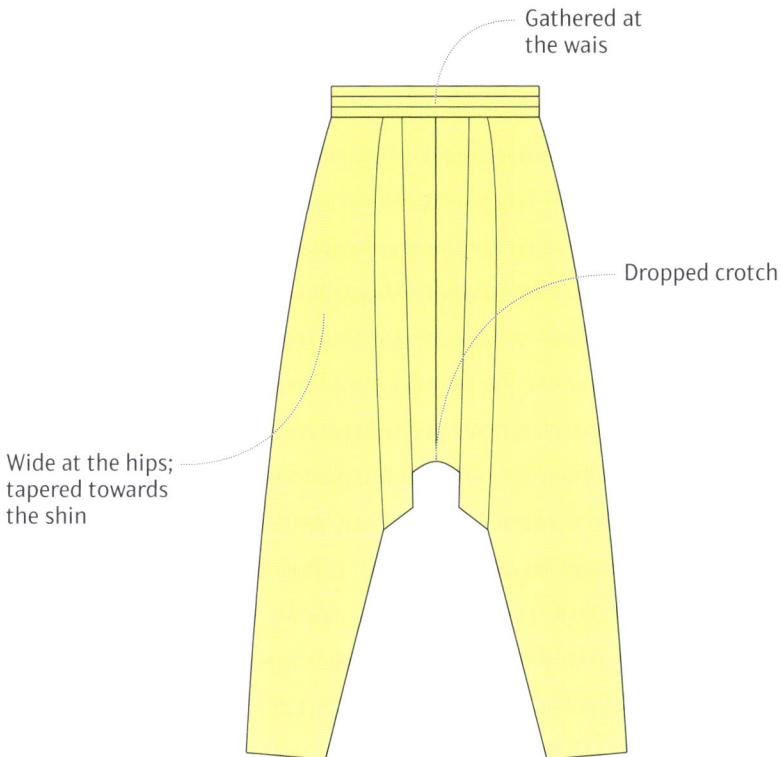

Gathered at
the wais

Dropped crotch

Wide at the hips;
tapered towards
the shin

Silk * Chiffon * Satin * Viscose * Knits * Cotton

243

Chinos

Originally part of the uniforms of British soldiers in India.

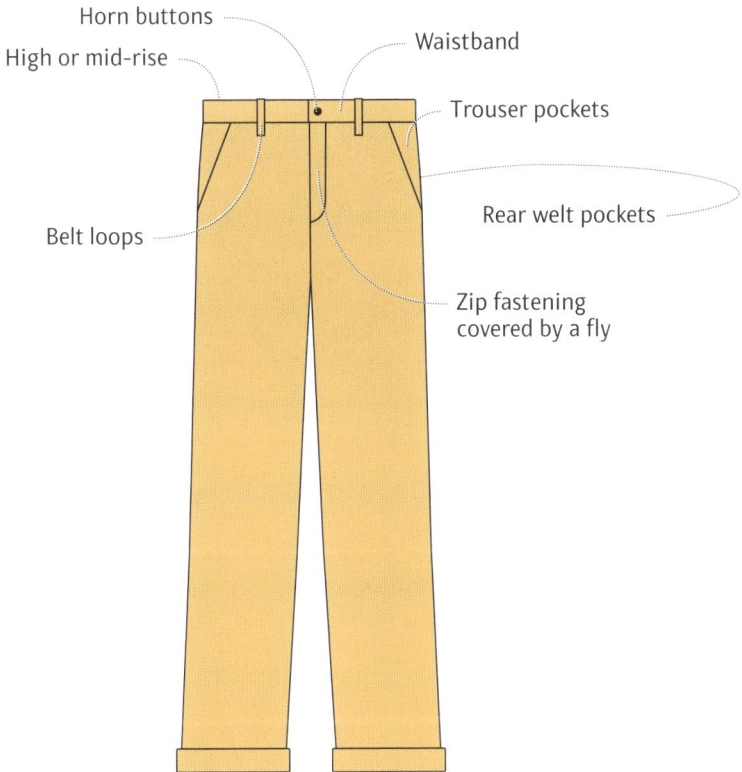

Horn buttons

High or mid-rise

Waistband

Trouser pockets

Belt loops

Rear welt pockets

Zip fastening
covered by a fly

* Cotton fabric with twill weave *

Leggins

Slim-fit elastic trousers.

No fasteners

No pockets

Skin tight fight

Skinny trousers

The defining attribute of the rebellious youth of the 1950s.

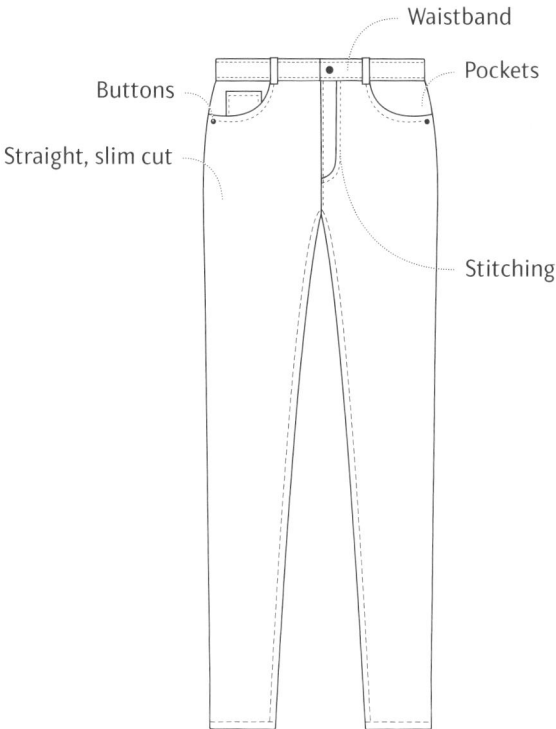

Waistband

Pockets

Buttons

Straight, slim cut

Stitching

* Cotton and elastane *

Drop-crotch trousers

Baggy, wide-leg trousers.

Low-rise

Waistband, covered
elastic or drawstring

Dropped crotch

Cuffs with or
without elastic

Linen * Leather * Denim * Cotton

Boiler suit

The original work uniform. One-piece garment,
also called overalls.

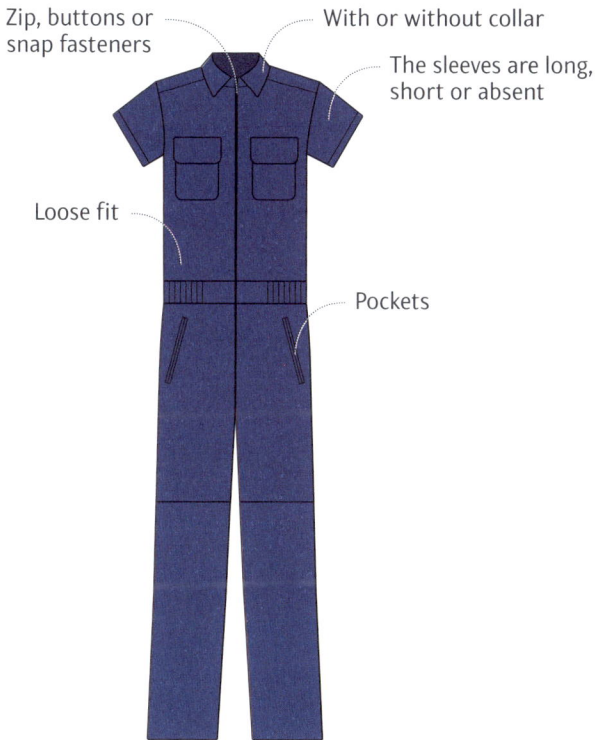

Zip, buttons or
snap fasteners

With or without collar

The sleeves are long,
short or absent

Loose fit

Pockets

Wool * Denim * Linen * Blended fabrics * Leather * Suede * Cotton

Skirts

Pleated skirt

Styles and details vary. Creases are created by pressing.

Waistband

Even creases,
narrow or wide

Varied lengths

Silk ∗ Knits ∗ Wool ∗ Linen ∗ Cotton

Wrap skirt

Waistband

Straight or trapezoid silhouette

Straight or asymmetrical hemline, with a vertical or diagonal overlapping panel

Knee to ankle-length

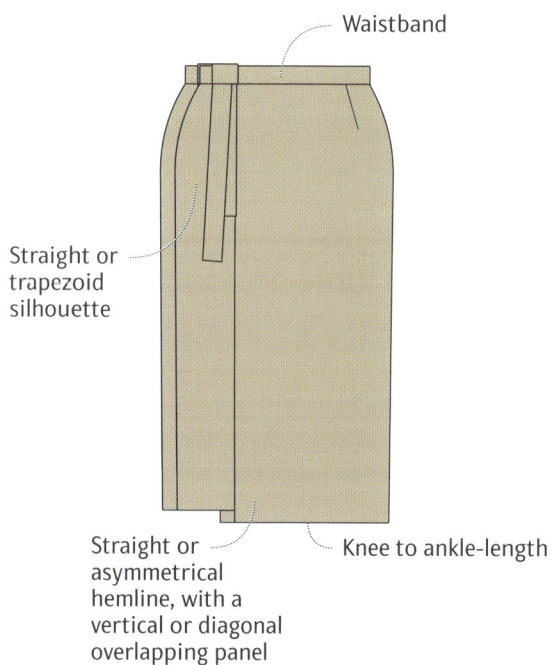

Denim ∗ Suiting fabric ∗ Leather
Jacquard ∗ Wool ∗ Cotton

Button front skirt

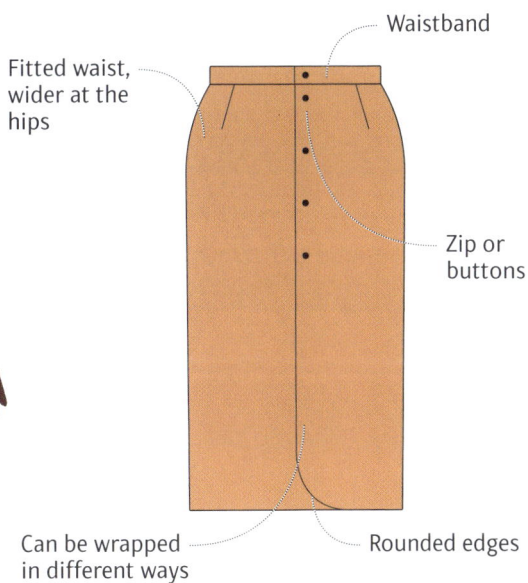

Fitted waist, wider at the hips

Waistband

Zip or buttons

Can be wrapped in different ways

Rounded edges

Denim * Suiting fabric * Leather
Jacquard * Wool * Cotton

Circle skirt

Skirt made from a single, round piece of fabric.

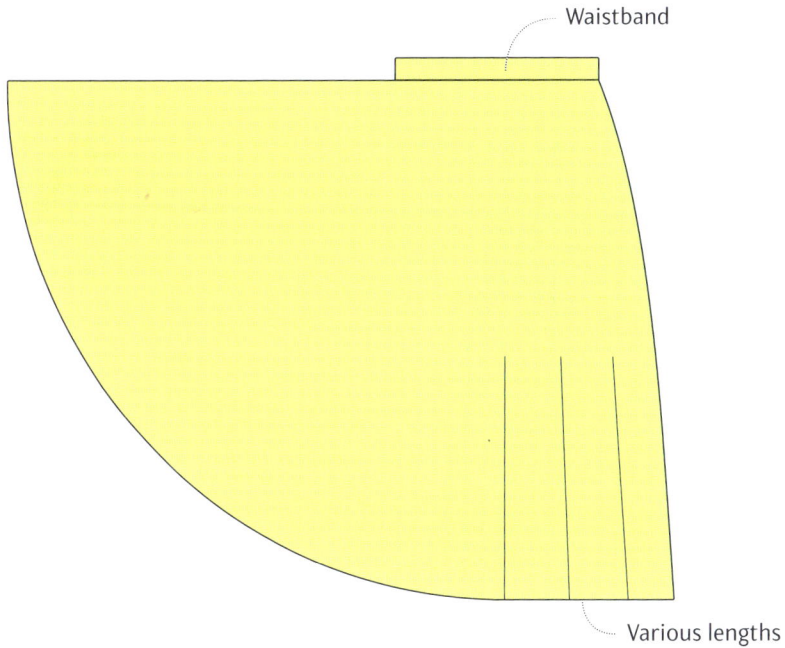

Waistband

Various lengths

Silk * Chiffon * Satin * Viscose * Knits * Cotton

Box pleat skirt

Pleats are closed
at the waist

Pleats extend
from the hips
to the hem

A line

Cotton * Linen * Wool * Leather
Dense knits

A line skirt

Fitted at the top

A line silhouette

Wider at the hem

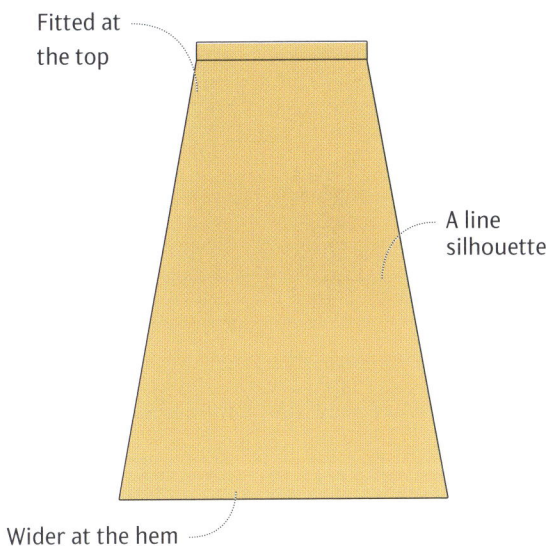

Cotton * Linen * Wool
Leather Denim * Batiste * Velvet
Chintz Jacquard * Knits

Tulip skirt

Similar to a trumpet skirt, this style is wider at the middle than the hem or waist, forming the shape of an upside-down tulip flower.

The shape of a tulip through simple pleats at the waist

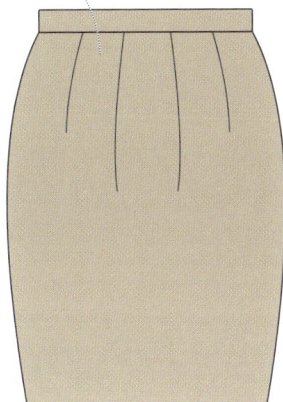

Short or elongated silhouette, slightly nipped in at the hem

* Fabric that holds its shape *

Pencil skirt

Slim knee-length skirt.

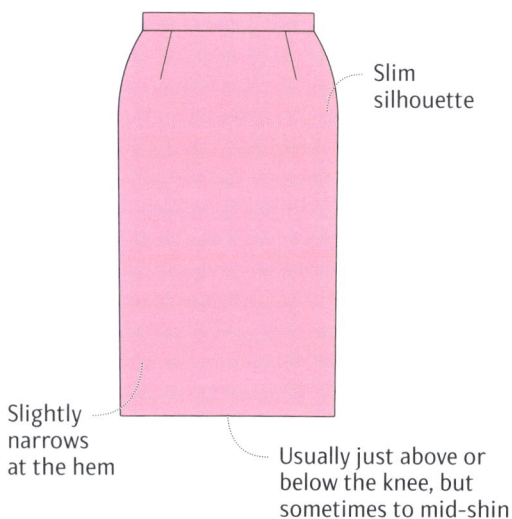

Slim
silhouette

Slightly
narrows
at the hem

Usually just above or
below the knee, but
sometimes to mid-shin

Crepe * Wool * Gabardine
Denim * Cotton * Linen * Dense
knit silk * Tweed * Corduroy

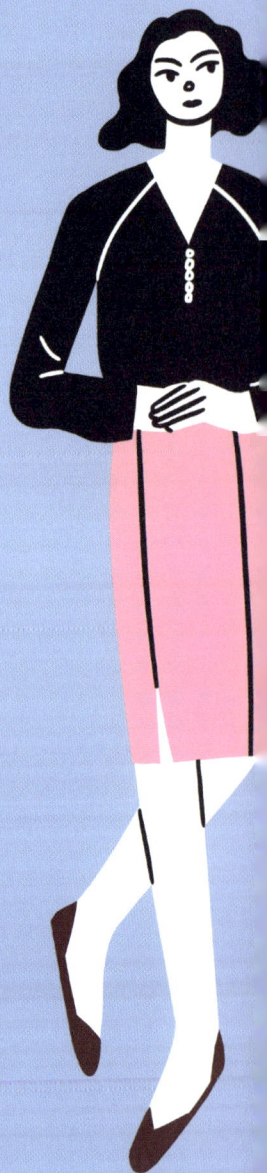

Miniskirt

Any short skirt.

Mid-thigh
or above

Crepe * Wool * Gabardine *
Denim * Cotton * Linen * Dense
knit silk * Tweed * Corduroy

Godet skirt

A flared skirt that uses triangular fabric
inserts to give the garment extra movement.

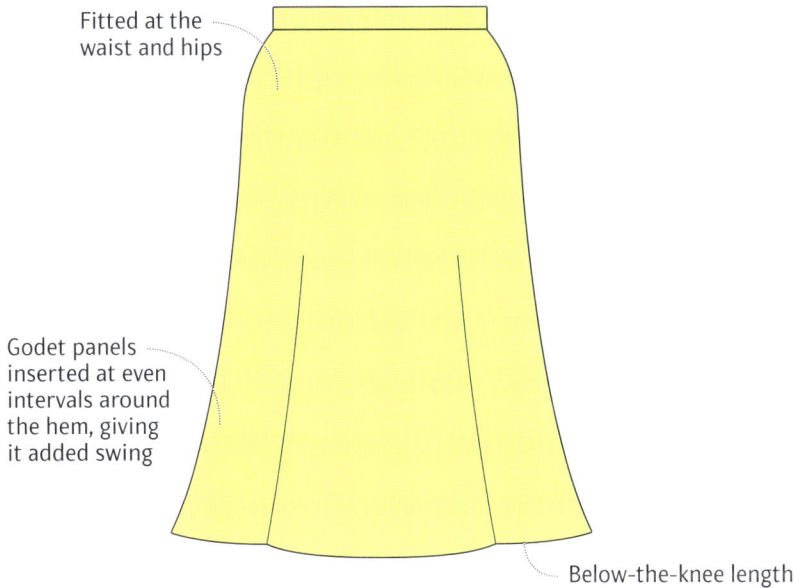

Fitted at the
waist and hips

Godet panels
inserted at even
intervals around
the hem, giving
it added swing

Below-the-knee length

Denim * Wool * Blended fabrics * Leather * Suede * Cotton

Index